Rolling Stone

EASY PIANO SHEET MUSIC CLASSICS VOLUME 2

34 SELECTIONS FROM THE

500 GREATEST SONGS OF ALL TIME

ARRANGED BY DAN COATES

Alfred Publishing Co., Inc.
16320 Roscoe Blvd., Suite 100
P.O. Box 10003
Van Nuys, CA 91410-0003
alfred.com

ISBN-10: 0-7390-5237-3
ISBN-13: 978-0-7390-5237-2

EASY PIANO SHEET MUSIC CLASSICS VOLUME 2

Rolling Stone® 500 Greatest Songs of All Time

Welcome to the ultimate jukebox: the *Rolling Stone* 500, a celebration of the greatest rock & roll songs of all time, chosen by a five-star jury of singers, musicians, producers, industry figures, critics and, of course, songwriters. The editors of *Rolling Stone* called on rock stars and leading authorities to list their fifty favorite songs, in order of preference. The 172 voters, who included Brian Wilson, Joni Mitchell and Wilco's Jeff Tweedy, were asked to select songs from the rock & roll era. They nominated 2,103 songs in virtually every pop-music genre of the past half-century and beyond, from Hank Williams to OutKast. The results were tabulated according to a weighted point system.

For this *RS* 500, the word *song* refers to both a composition and its definitive recorded performance, as a single or an album track. Bob Dylan, the Beatles and the Rolling Stones accounted for a combined total of 117 nominated songs, a measure of their unbroken reign as rock's most influential, beloved artists. Nirvana and the Clash crashed the top twenty, rubbing guitars with Chuck Berry and Jimi Hendrix.

This *RS* 500 is also a tribute to the eternal power of popular music, and great songwriting in particular, to reflect and transform the times in which we hear it. The *RS* 500 salutes the songs that move us—and the artists who create them. It is also proof that whenever you want to know what's going on, listen to the music.

ARTIST INDEX

CONTENTS

CONTENTS

All I Have to Do Is Dream
The Everly Brothers

Written by: Boudleaux and Felice Bryant
Produced by: Archie Bleyer
Released: May '58 on Cadence
Charts: 11 weeks; top spot no. 21

›› **No. 141** *from Rolling Stone® Magazine's 500 Greatest Songs of All Time*

Although Don Everly had a contract to work as a songwriter before he and his brother Phil began their hitmaking, their first three big singles were all written by the husband-and-wife team of Boudleaux and Felice Bryant. "I would go to them for lovelorn advice when I was young and divorce advice when I was older," Phil said. "All I Have to Do Is Dream," with Chet Atkins' innovative tremolo chording backing the brothers' high-lonesome harmonies, went to Number One on not just the pop chart but the R&B chart as well.

Appears on: All-Time Original Hits (Rhino)
(Music appears on page 14)

Billie Jean
Michael Jackson

Written by: Jackson
Produced by: Jackson, Quincy Jones
Released: Jan. '83 on Epic
Charts: 7 weeks; top spot no. 1

›› **No. 58** *from Rolling Stone® Magazine's 500 Greatest Songs of All Time*

Sinuous, paranoid and omnipresent: the single that made Jackson the biggest star since Elvis was a denial of a paternity suit, and it spent seven weeks at Number One. Jackson came up with the irresistible rhythm track on his home drum machine and nailed the vocals in one take. "I knew it was going to be big while I was writing it," he said. "I was really absorbed in writing it." How absorbed? He was thinking about the song while riding in his Rolls down the Ventura Freeway in California – and didn't notice the car was on fire.

Appears on: Thriller (Sony)
(Music appears on page 17)

Blueberry Hill
Fats Domino

Written by: Al Lewis, Larry Stock, Vincent Rose
Produced by: Dave Bartholomew
Released: Oct. '56 on Imperial
Charts: 27 weeks; top spot no. 2

›› **No. 81** *from Rolling Stone® Magazine's 500 Greatest Songs of All Time*

"Blueberry Hill" was first done by Gene Autry in 1940. But Domino drew on the 1949 Louis Armstrong version when he had run out of material at a session. Producer Bartholomew thought it was a terrible idea but lost the argument. Good thing, too. It ended up being Domino's biggest hit and broadened his audience once and for all. As Carl Perkins later said, "In the white honky-tonks where I was playin', they were punchin' 'Blueberry Hill.' And white cats were dancin' to Fats Domino."

Appears on: The Fats Domino Jukebox (Capitol)
(Music appears on page 22)

Born to Run
Bruce Springsteen

Written by: Springsteen
Produced by: Springsteen, Mike Appel
Released: Aug. '75 on Columbia
Charts: 11 weeks; top spot no. 23

›› **No. 21** *from Rolling Stone® Magazine's 500 Greatest Songs of All Time*

This song's four and a half minutes took three and a half months to cut. Aiming for the impact of Phil Spector's Wall of Sound, Springsteen included strings, glockenspiel, multiple keyboards – and more than a dozen guitar tracks. The words poured out just as relentlessly, telling a story of young lovers on the highways of New Jersey. "I don't know how important the settings are in the first place," Springsteen told *Rolling Stone*. "It's the idea behind the settings. It could be New Jersey, it could be California, it could be Alaska."

Appears on: Born to Run (Columbia)
(Music appears on page 25)

The Boxer
Simon and Garfunkel

Written by: Paul Simon
Produced by: Roy Halee, Simon, Art Garfunkel
Released: April '69 on Columbia
Charts: 10 weeks; top spot no. 7

›› **No. 105** *from Rolling Stone® Magazine's 500 Greatest Songs of All Time*

One of Simon and Garfunkel's most enduring songs, "The Boxer" is about a New York kid who can't find love, a job or a home – just those old whores on

Seventh Avenue. "I think I was reading the Bible," Simon said of the song's genesis. "That's where [the line] 'workman's wages' came from." Simon famously performed the song on the first *Saturday Night Live* after 9/11, as a tribute to New York's resilience.

Appears on: Bridge Over Troubled Water (Columbia)

(Music appears on page 32)

Desperado
Eagles

Written by: Glenn Frey, Don Henley
Produced by: Bill Szymczyk
Released: April '73 on Asylum
Charts: Non-single

»**No. 494** *from Rolling Stone® Magazine's 500 Greatest Songs of All Time*

"Desperado" was the title track of the Eagles' second LP, a concept album about outlaws in the Old West. "In retrospect, I admit the whole cowboy-outlaw-rocker myth was a bit bogus," Henley said in 1987. "I don't think we really believed it; we were just trying to make an analogy."

Appears on: Desperado (Elektra)

(Music appears on page 38)

Earth Angel
The Penguins

Written by: Jesse Belvin, Curtis Williams
Produced by: Dootsie Williams
Released: Dec. '54 on Dootone
Charts: 15 weeks; top spot no. 8

»**No. 151** *from Rolling Stone® Magazine's 500 Greatest Songs of All Time*

Crudely recorded in a garage and released on a small label, "Earth Angel" turned out to be a pivotal record in rock & roll's early development. The artless, unaffected vocals of the Penguins, four black high schoolers from L.A., defined the street-corner elegance of doo-wop. The Penguins' version also outsold a sanitized, big-label cover by schmaltzy white group the Crew-Cuts.

Appears on: Earth Angel (Ace)

(Music appears on page 42)

Fake Plastic Trees
Radiohead

Written by: Radiohead
Produced by: John Leckie

Released: March '95 on Capitol
Charts: 4 weeks; top spot no. 65

»**No. 376** *from Rolling Stone® Magazine's 500 Greatest Songs of All Time*

Radiohead frontman Thom Yorke would describe "Fake Plastic Trees" as the song on which he found his lyrical voice. He cut the vocal, accompanying himself on acoustic guitar, in one take, then the band filled in its parts around him. Yorke said the song began as "a very nice melody which I had no idea what to do with, then you wake up and find your head singing some words to it."

Appears on: The Bends (Capitol)

(Music appears on page 45)

Great Balls of Fire
Jerry Lee Lewis

Written by: Otis Blackwell, Jack Hammer
Produced by: Sam Phillips
Released: Nov. '57 on Sun
Charts: 21 weeks; top spot no. 2

»**No. 96** *from Rolling Stone® Magazine's 500 Greatest Songs of All Time*

With Lewis pounding the piano and leering, "Great Balls of Fire" was full of Southern Baptist hellfire turned into a near-blasphemous ode to pure lust. Lewis, a Bible-college dropout and cousin to Jimmy Swaggart, refused to sing it at first and got into a theological argument with Phillips that concluded with Lewis asking, "How can the devil save souls?" But as the session wore on and the liquor kept flowing, Lewis' mood changed considerably – on bootleg tapes he can be heard saying, "I would like to eat a little pussy if I had some." Goodness gracious, great balls of fire, indeed.

Appears on: Original Sun Greatest Hits (Rhino)

(Music appears on page 50)

I Can See for Miles
The Who

Written by: Pete Townshend
Produced by: Kit Lambert
Released: Oct. '67 on Decca
Charts: 11 weeks; top spot no. 9

»**No. 258** *from Rolling Stone® Magazine's 500 Greatest Songs of All Time*

"I sat down and made it good from the beginning," Townshend said of the Who's most volcanic studio single in his first *Rolling Stone* interview. Written in

1966, "Miles" was painstakingly built in London and L.A. on rare days off from touring in the summer of '67, with Townshend piling on multiple guitars to replicate his onstage amp howl. That fury powered the song into the U.S. Top Ten.

Appears on: _The Who Sell Out_ (MCA)

(Music appears on page 53)

I Got You Babe
Sonny and Cher

Written by: Sonny Bono
Produced by: Bono
Released: July '65 on Atco
Charts: 14 weeks; top spot no. 1

>>**No. 444** _from Rolling Stone® Magazine's 500 Greatest Songs of All Time_

Sonny and Cher were living in their manager's house, where Bono would go down to the garage and bang out songs all night on an upright piano. One night, he woke up Cher and asked her to listen to his latest tune, "I Got You Babe," and sing the lyrics, which he had written on a piece of shirt cardboard. She thought it was OK but really wanted a song that modulated. So Bono changed the key at the bridge and woke Cher up once again hours later to hear it; she was delighted. Sonny and Cher had their first Top Forty hit, and their only Number One record.

Appears on: _The Beat Goes On: The Best of Sonny and Cher_ (Atlantic)

(Music appears on page 58)

I Wanna Be Sedated
Ramones

Written by: Ramones
Produced by: Tommy Erdelyi, Ed Stasium
Released: Oct. '78 on Sire
Charts: Did not chart

>>**No. 144** _from Rolling Stone® Magazine's 500 Greatest Songs of All Time_

The greatest God-does-the-road-ever-suck song, "I Wanna Be Sedated" was written by Joey Ramone, who at the time was suffering from severe teakettle burns and had to fly to London for a gig. Plagued by obsessive-compulsive disorder and various other ailments, Joey always had a rough time touring. "Put me in a wheelchair/And get me to the show/Hurry hurry hurry/Before I go loco!" he rants. The sound is equally pissed-off: Johnny's guitar solo – the same note,

sixty-five times in a row – is the ultimate expression of his anti-artifice philosophy; the bubblegum-pop key change that follows it, though, is pure Joey.

Appears on: _Road to Ruin_ (Rhino)

(Music appears on page 62)

I Want to Hold Your Hand
The Beatles

Written by: John Lennon, Paul McCartney
Produced by: George Martin
Released: Dec. '63 on Capitol
Charts: 15 weeks; top spot no. 1

>>**No. 16** _from Rolling Stone® Magazine's 500 Greatest Songs of All Time_

In 1963, the Beatles issued an ultimatum. "We said to [manager] Brian Epstein, 'We're not going to America till we've got a Number One record,' " Paul McCartney said. So he and John Lennon went to the home of the parents of Jane Asher, McCartney's girlfriend, where they – "one on one, eyeball to eyeball," as Lennon said – wrote "I Want to Hold Your Hand," a complex series of mood and chord changes packed into a lighting bolt of infatuation. The energy of their collaboration ran through the band's performance, taped October 17th, 1963. On February 7th, 1964, the Beatles landed in New York the way they wanted: top of the pops.

Appears on: _1_ (Apple/Capitol)

(Music appears on page 66)

In My Room
The Beach Boys

Written by: Brian Wilson, Gary Usher
Produced by: Wilson
Released: Sept. '63 on Capitol
Charts: 11 weeks; top spot no. 23

>>**No. 209** _from Rolling Stone® Magazine's 500 Greatest Songs of All Time_

Though Usher wrote the lyrics, the song's conceit was pure Wilson. "Brian was always saying that his room was his whole world," Usher said. The three-part harmony on the first verse that Wilson sang with his brothers Carl and Dennis recalled the vocal bits that Brian taught them when they shared a childhood bedroom. As the Beatles had done with some hits, the Boys cut a version in German.

Appears on: _Surfer Girl/Shut Down, Volume 2_ (Capitol)

(Music appears on page 74)

Knocking on Heaven's Door
Bob Dylan

Written by: Dylan
Produced by: Gordon Carroll
Released: July '73 on Columbia
Charts: 16 weeks; top spot no. 12

»**No. 190** *from Rolling Stone® Magazine's 500 Greatest Songs of All Time*

Three years had passed since his last studio album, and Dylan seemed at a loss. So he accepted an invitation to go to Mexico for Sam Peckinpah's *Pat Garrett and Billy the Kid,* for which he shot a bit part and did the soundtrack. For a death scene, Dylan delivered this tale of a dying sheriff, who wants only to lay his "guns in the ground."

Appears on: *The Essential Bob Dylan* (Sony)
(Music appears on page 78)

Like a Rolling Stone
Bob Dylan

Written by: Dylan
Produced by: Tom Wilson
Released: July '65 on Columbia
Charts: 12 weeks; top spot no. 2

»**No. 1** *from Rolling Stone® Magazine's 500 Greatest Songs of All Time*

"I wrote it. I didn't fail. It was straight," Bob Dylan said of his greatest song shortly after he wrote and recorded it in June 1965. There is no better description of "Like a Rolling Stone" – of its revolutionary design and execution – or of the young man, just turned twenty-four, who created it.

Al Kooper, who played organ on the session, remembers today, "There was no sheet music, it was totally by ear. And it was totally disorganized, totally punk. It just happened."

To this day, the most stunning thing about "Like a Rolling Stone" is the abundance of precedent: the impressionist voltage of Dylan's language, the intensely personal accusation in his voice (*"Ho-o-o-ow does it fe-e-e-el?"*), the apocalyptic charge of Kooper's garage-gospel organ and Mike Bloomfield's stiletto-sharp spirals of Telecaster guitar, the defiant six-minute length of the June 16th master take. No other pop song has so thoroughly challenged and transformed the commercial laws and artistic conventions of its time, for all time.

During his British tour in May 1965, immortalized in D.A. Pennebaker's documentary *Don't Look Back,* Dylan began writing an extended piece of verse – twenty pages long by one account, six in another – that was, he said, "just a rhythm thing on paper all about my steady hatred, directed at some point that was honest." Back home in Woodstock, New York, over three days in early June, Dylan sharpened the sprawl down to that confrontational chorus and four taut verses bursting with piercing metaphor and concise truth. "The first two lines, which rhymed 'kiddin' you' and 'didn't you,' just about knocked me out," he confessed to *Rolling Stone* in 1988, "and later on, when I got to the jugglers and the chrome horse and the princess on the steeple, it all just about got to be too much."

The beginnings of "Like a Rolling Stone" – and its roots in Dylan's earliest musical loves – can be seen in a pair of offstage moments in *Don't Look Back.* In the first, sidekick Bob Neuwirth gets Dylan to sing a verse of Hank Williams' "Lost Highway," which begins, "I'm a rolling stone, I'm alone and lost/For a life of sin I've paid the cost." Later, Dylan sits at a piano, playing a set of chords that would become the melodic basis for "Like a Rolling Stone," connecting it to the fundamental architecture of rock & roll. Dylan later identified that progression as a chip off of Ritchie Valens' "La Bamba."

Yet Dylan obsessed over the forward march in "Like a Rolling Stone." Before going into Columbia Records' New York studios to cut it, he summoned Bloomfield, the guitarist in the Paul Butterfield Blues Band, to Woodstock to learn the song. "He said, 'I don't want you to play any of that B.B. King shit, none of that fucking blues,'" recalled Bloomfield (who died in 1981). "I want you to play something else." Dylan later said much the same thing to the rest of the studio band, which included pianist Paul Griffin, bassist Russ Savakus and drummer Bobby Gregg: "I told them how to play on it, and if they didn't want to play it like that, well, they couldn't play with me."

Just as Dylan bent folk music's roots and forms to his own will, he transformed popular song with the content and ambition of "Like a Rolling Stone." And in his electrifying vocal performance, his best on record, Dylan proved that everything he did was, first and always, rock & roll. " 'Rolling Stone''s the best song I wrote," he said flatly at the end of 1965. It still is.

Appears on: *Highway 61 Revisited* (Columbia)
(Music appears on page 69)

Love Me Tender
Elvis Presley

Written by: Presley, Vera Watson
Produced by: Steve Sholes
Released: Oct. '56 on RCA
Charts: 23 weeks; top spot no. 1

»**No. 437** *from Rolling Stone® Magazine's 500 Greatest Songs of All Time*

"Love Me Tender" was the theme song from the first Elvis movie. It also represented a brand-new sound for the King. He sang in his softest voice, accompanied only by his own acoustic guitar. The melody came from the Civil War-era ballad "Aura Lee," adapted by the movie's musical director, Ken Darby, who gave credit to Watson, his wife.

Appears on: Elvis 30 #1 Hits (RCA)

(Music appears on page 80)

Maggie May
Rod Stewart

Written by: Stewart, Martin Quittenton
Produced by: Stewart
Released: June '71 on Mercury
Charts: 17 weeks; top spot no. 1

»**No. 130** *from Rolling Stone® Magazine's 500 Greatest Songs of All Time*

Stewart plays a schoolboy in love with an older temptress in "Maggie May," trying desperately to subdue his hormones with common sense. The song was a last-minute addition to the LP *Every Picture Tells a Story* and was initially the B side of "Reason to Believe." Stewart has joked that if a DJ hadn't flipped the single over, he'd have gone back to his old job: digging graves. But the song's rustic country mandolin and acoustic guitars – and Mickey Waller's simple but relentless drum-bashing – were undeniable.

Appears on: Every Picture Tells a Story (Mercury/Universal)

(Music appears on page 82)

O-o-h Child
The Five Stairsteps

Written by: Stan Vincent
Produced by: Vincent
Released: April '70 on Buddah
Charts: 16 weeks; top spot no. 8

»**No. 392** *from Rolling Stone® Magazine's 500 Greatest Songs of All Time*

"O-o-h Child" gave the Five Stairsteps – four brothers and a sister from Chicago – a pop-soul classic that rivaled the hits of another sibling gang, the Jackson 5. The children of police detective Clarence Burke, the Five Stairsteps, who played their own music as well as sang, ranged in age from thirteen to seventeen when Curtis Mayfield signed them to his Windy C label.

Appears on: Soul Hits of the '70s: Didn't It Blow Your Mind! Vol. 2 (Rhino)

(Music appears on page 86)

Paint It, Black
The Rolling Stones

Written by: Mick Jagger, Keith Richards
Produced by: Andrew Oldham
Released: May '66 on London
Charts: 11 weeks; top spot no. 1

»**No. 174** *from Rolling Stone® Magazine's 500 Greatest Songs of All Time*

Brian Jones plucked the haunting sitar melody at the 1966 L.A. session for this classic. Bill Wyman added klezmer-flavored organ; studio legend Jack Nitzsche played the gypsy-style piano. "Brian had pretty much given up on the guitar by then," said Richards. "If there was [another] instrument around, he had to be able to get something out of it. It gave the Stones on record a lot of different textures."

Appears on: Aftermath (ABKCO)

(Music appears on page 91)

People Get Ready
The Impressions

Written by: Curtis Mayfield
Produced by: Johnny Pate
Released: Jan. '65 on ABC-Paramount
Charts: 8 weeks; top spot no. 14

»**No. 24** *from Rolling Stone® Magazine's 500 Greatest Songs of All Time*

"It was warrior music," said civil-rights activist Gordon Sellers. "It was music you listened to while you were preparing to go into battle." Mayfield wrote the gospel-driven R&B ballad, he said, "in a deep mood, a spiritual state of mind," just before Martin Luther King's march on the group's hometown of Chicago. Shortly after "People Get Ready" was released, Chicago churches began including their own version of it in songbooks.

Mayfield had ended the song with "You don't need no ticket/You just thank the Lord," but the church version, ironically, made it less Christian and more universal: "Everybody wants freedom/This I know."

Appears on: *The Very Best of the Impressions* (Rhino)

(Music appears on page 96)

(We're Gonna) Rock Around the Clock
Bill Haley and His Comets

Written by: Jimmy DeKnight, Max Freedman
Produced by: Milt Gabler
Released: May '54 on Decca
Charts: 24 weeks; top spot no. 1

»No. 158 *from Rolling Stone® Magazine's 500 Greatest Songs of All Time*

Haley started as a country yodeler but converted to rock & roll when he saw how it moved his audiences. "Rock" was a modest success until it played during the opening credits of *The Blackboard Jungle* and shot to Number One.

Appears on: *The Best of Bill Haley and His Comets* (MCA)

(Music appears on page 102)

Sail Away
Randy Newman

Written by: Newman
Produced by: Lenny Waronker
Released: June '72 on Reprise
Charts: Did not chart

»No. 264 *from Rolling Stone® Magazine's 500 Greatest Songs of All Time*

Everybody from Ray Charles to Etta James has covered this piano ballad – even though it's a portrait of America from the perspective of a slave trader. As usual for Newman, it combines lush melody with painfully funny satire. "One thing with my music," Newman admitted, "you can't sit and eat potato chips and have it on in the background at a party."

Appears on: *Sail Away* (Rhino)

(Music appears on page 104)

Save the Last Dance for Me
The Drifters

Written by: Doc Pomus, Mort Shuman
Produced by: Jerry Leiber, Mike Stoller
Released: Sept. '60 on Atlantic
Charts: 18 weeks; top spot no. 1

»No. 182 *from Rolling Stone® Magazine's 500 Greatest Songs of All Time*

Billy Joel said it best: Before the Drifters, the last dance was the one nobody stuck around for. But this elegant R&B ballad made the end of the party sound like the essence of true romance. Lead vocalist Ben E. King later sang the solo hit "Stand By Me."

Appears on: *The Drifters' Golden Hits* (Atlantic)

(Music appears on page 99)

Sh-Boom
The Chords

Written by: James Edwards, Carl Feaster, Claude Feaster, James Keyes, Floyd McRae
Produced by: Ahmet Ertegun
Released: April '54 on Cat
Charts: Predates pop charts

»No. 215 *from Rolling Stone® Magazine's 500 Greatest Songs of All Time*

"Life could be a dream.... If you would tell me I'm the only one that you love," sang the Chords in this doo-wop hit. Some music historians consider this to be the first rock & roll record. Said Keyes, the group's first tenor, "[Our voices] were like horns blowing rhythmic things." The "boom" in the title chorus was inspired by the then-raging fear of the H-bomb.

Appears on: *Doo Wop Box* (Rhino)

(Music appears on page 108)

The Sound of Silence
Simon and Garfunkel

Written by: Paul Simon
Produced by: Tom Wilson
Released: Nov. '65 on Columbia
Charts: 14 weeks; top spot no. 1

»No. 156 *from Rolling Stone® Magazine's 500 Greatest Songs of All Time*

Simon wrote this as an acoustic ballad, but Simon and Garfunkel's first single version died. While Simon was in England, Wilson, who was producing Bob Dylan's "Like a Rolling Stone," asked members of Dylan's studio band to add electric guitar and drums to Simon's song. Columbia released the amplified "Silence," which became a hit before Simon and Garfunkel had even heard it.

Appears on: Sounds of Silence (Columbia)

(Music appears on page 112)

Stairway to Heaven
Led Zeppelin

Written by: Jimmy Page, Robert Plant
Produced by: Page
Released: Nov. '71 on Atlantic
Charts: Non-single

»No. 31 *from Rolling Stone® Magazine's 500 Greatest Songs of All Time*

All epic anthems must measure themselves against "Stairway to Heaven," the cornerstone of *Led Zeppelin IV*. Building from an acoustic intro that sounds positively Elizabethan, thanks to John Paul Jones' recorder solo and Plant's fanciful lyrics, it morphs into a Page solo that storms heaven's gate. Page said the song "crystallized the essence of the band. It had everything there and showed the band at its best.... as a band, as a unit.... It was a milestone for us. Every musician wants to do something of lasting quality, something which will hold up for a long time, and I guess we did it with 'Stairway.' "

Appears on: Led Zeppelin IV (Atlantic)

(Music appears on page 117)

Stand By Me
Ben E. King

Written by: King, Elmo Glick, Jerry Leiber, Mike Stoller
Produced by: Leiber, Stoller
Released: April '61 on Atco
Charts: 14 weeks; top spot no. 4

»No. 121 *from Rolling Stone® Magazine's 500 Greatest Songs of All Time*

King wrote "Stand By Me" when he was still the lead singer of the Drifters – but the group didn't want it. As King recalled, the Drifters' manager told him, "Not a bad song, but we don't need it." But after King went solo, he revived "Stand By Me" at the end of a session with Leiber. "I showed him the song," King said. "Did it on piano a little bit. He called the musicians back into the studio, and we went ahead and recorded it." "Stand By Me" has been a classic ever since.

Appears on: The Very Best of Ben E. King (Rhino)

(Music appears on page 122)

Stayin' Alive
Bee Gees

Written by: Robin Gibb, Barry Gibb, Maurice Gibb
Produced by: Barry Gibb, Robin Gibb, Maurice Gibb, Karl Richardson, Albhy Galuten
Released: Nov. '77 on RSO
Charts: 27 weeks; top spot no. 1

»No. 189 *from Rolling Stone® Magazine's 500 Greatest Songs of All Time*

This disco classic was written after Robert Stigwood asked the Bee Gees for music for a film he was producing based on a *New York* magazine account of the Brooklyn club scene.

Appears on: Saturday Night Fever (Polydor)

(Music appears on page 126)

Wake Up Little Susie
The Everly Brothers

Written by: Felice Bryant, Boudleaux Bryant
Produced by: Archie Bleyer
Released: Sept. '57 on Cadence
Charts: 26 weeks; top spot no. 1

»No. 311 *from Rolling Stone® Magazine's 500 Greatest Songs of All Time*

Though it sounds quaint today, "Wake Up Little Susie," the tale of a teen couple who fall asleep at a drive-in, stirred up controversy in 1957. The song was banned in Boston but became the Everlys' first Number One. In 2000, when candidate George W. Bush was asked by Oprah Winfrey what his favorite song was, he said, " 'Wake Up Little Susie,' by Buddy Holly."

Appears on: The Best of the Every Brothers (Rhino)

(Music appears on page 130)

The Weight
The Band

Written by: Robbie Robertson
Produced by: John Simon
Released: Aug. '68 on Capitol
Charts: 7 weeks; top spot no. 63

>>**No. 41** *from Rolling Stone® Magazine's 500 Greatest Songs of All Time*

The Band was chiefly known as Bob Dylan's touring group when it retreated to a pink house in Woodstock, New York, to record its debut, *Music From Big Pink*. The homespun album was centered by "The Weight," an oddball fable of debt and burden. Robertson said he was inspired to write the song after watching Spanish director Luis Buñuel's films about "the impossibility of sainthood," but characters such as Crazy Chester could have walked straight out of an old folk song. As for the biblical-sounding line "pulled into Nazareth," it refers to Nazareth, Pennsylvania, home of the Martin Guitar factory.

Appears on: Music From Big Pink *(Capitol)*

(Music appears on page 146)

White Room
Cream

Written by: Pete Brown, Jack Bruce
Produced by: Felix Pappalardi
Released: Aug. '68 on Atco
Charts: 11 weeks; top spot no. 6

>>**No. 367** *from Rolling Stone® Magazine's 500 Greatest Songs of All Time*

The song's unnerving psychedelic imagery came from lyricist Brown, who had just gone through a period of drug and alcohol excess. "It was in my white-painted room that I had the horrible drug experience that made me want to stop everything," he said.

Appears on: Wheels of Fire *(Polygram)*

(Music appears on page 134)

A Whiter Shade of Pale
Procol Harum

Written by: Keith Reid, Gary Brooker
Produced by: Denny Cordell
Released: June '67 on A&M
Charts: 12 weeks; top spot no. 5

>>**No. 57** *from Rolling Stone® Magazine's 500 Greatest Songs of All Time*

A somber hymn supported by an organ theme straight out of Bach ("Air on the G String," from the "Suite No. 3 in D Major"), Procol Harum's "A Whiter Shade of Pale" was unlike anything on the radio in 1967. It was also the only track recorded by the initial lineup of Procol Harum, which started as an R&B band, the Paramounts, in 1963. A worldwide smash that sold more than 6 million copies and quickly found its way into wedding ceremonies (and, later, the *Big Chill* soundtrack), "Pale" helped kick-start the classical-rock boomlet that gave the world the Moody Blues.

Appears on: Greatest Hits *(A&M)*

(Music appears on page 138)

Will You Love Me Tomorrow
The Shirelles

Written by: Gerry Goffin, Carole King
Produced by: Luther Dixon
Released: Nov. '60 on Scepter
Charts: 19 weeks; top spot no. 1

>>**No. 125** *from Rolling Stone® Magazine's 500 Greatest Songs of All Time*

After a few minor Shirelles hits, Scepter Records founder Florence Greenberg asked King and Goffin to write the group a song. On the piano in Greenberg's office, King finished a song the team had been working on: "Will You Love Me Tomorrow." "I remember giving her baby a bottle while Carole was writing the song," Greenberg said. Lead singer Shirley Owens initially found the song too countryish for the group, but Dixon's production changed her mind and made it the first Number One for a girl group.

Appears on: Girl Group Greats *(Rhino)*

(Music appears on page 142)

ALL I HAVE TO DO IS DREAM

Words and Music by Boudleaux Bryant
Arranged by Dan Coates

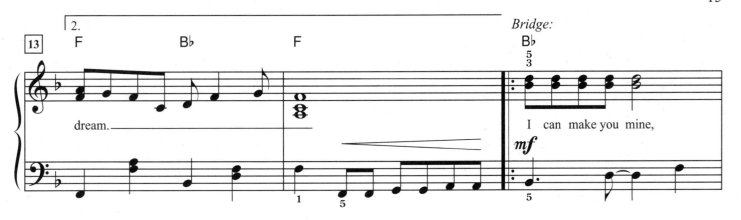

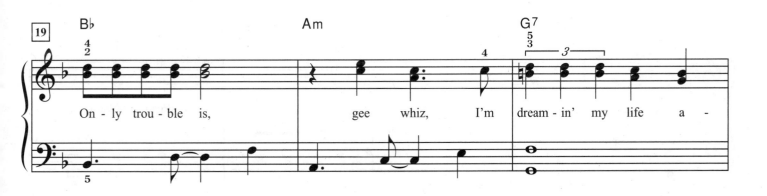

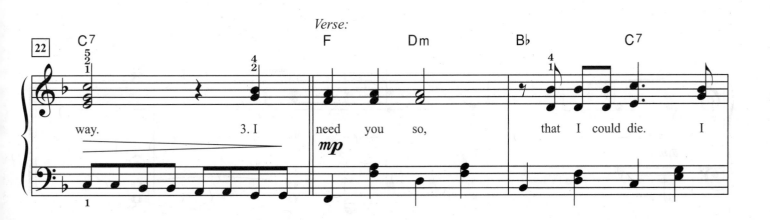

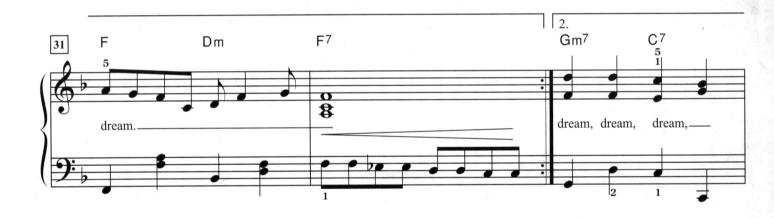

BILLIE JEAN

Written and Composed by Michael Jackson
Arranged by Dan Coates

Moderately, with a steady rock beat

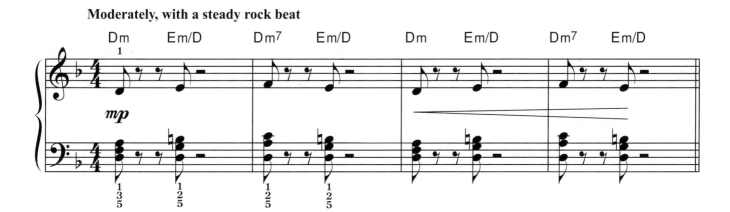

Verse:

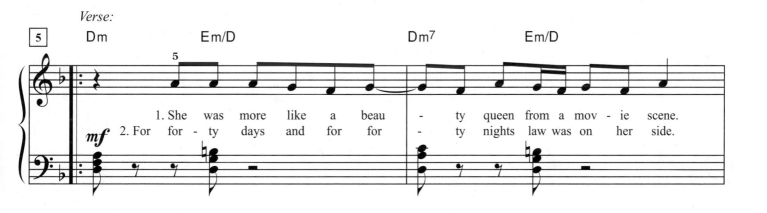

1. She was more like a beau - ty queen from a mov - ie scene.
2. For for - ty days and for for - ty nights law was on her side.

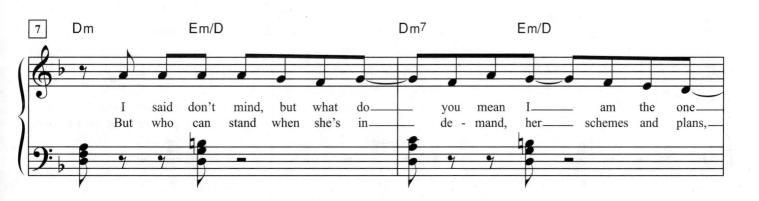

I said don't mind, but what do you mean I am the one
But who can stand when she's in de - mand, her schemes and plans,

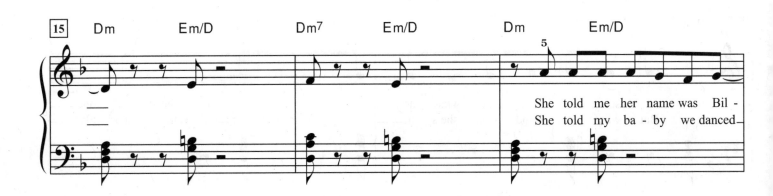

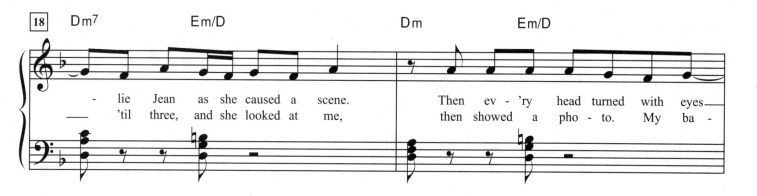

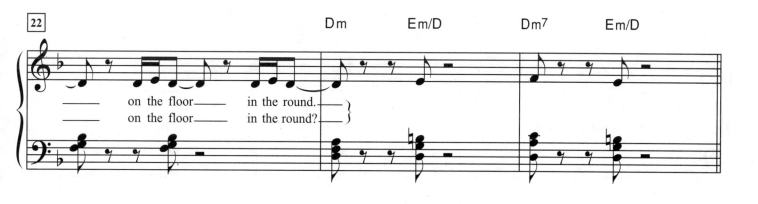

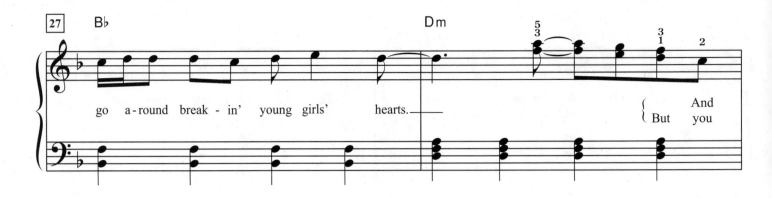

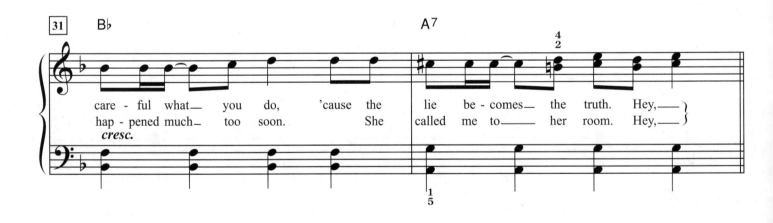

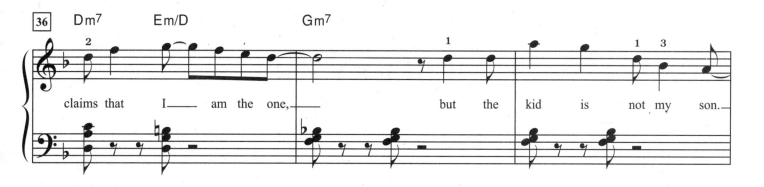

claims that I___ am the one,___ but the kid is not my son.___

___ She says I___ am the one,___ but the

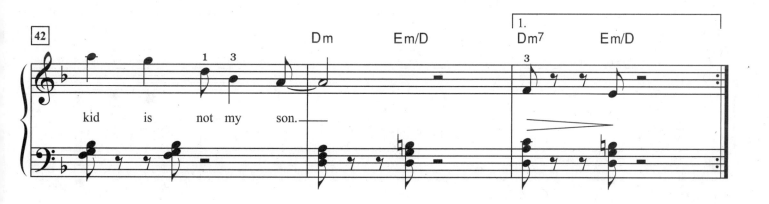

kid is not my son.___

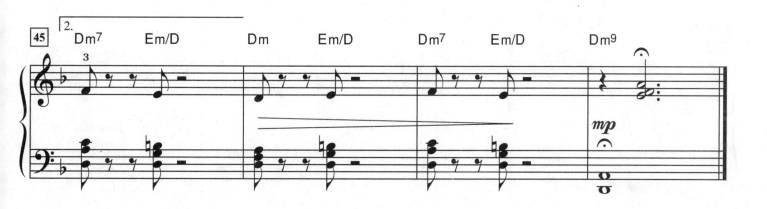

BLUEBERRY HILL

Words and Music by
Al Lewis, Vincent Rose and Larry Stock
Arranged by Dan Coates

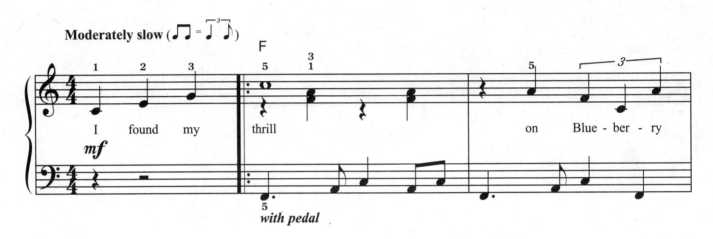

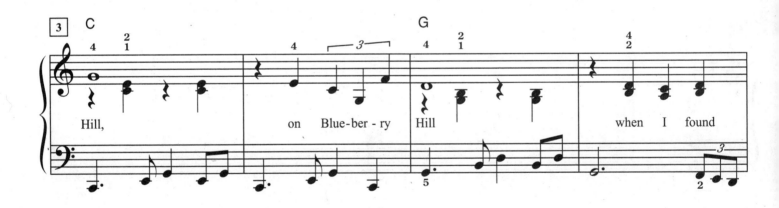

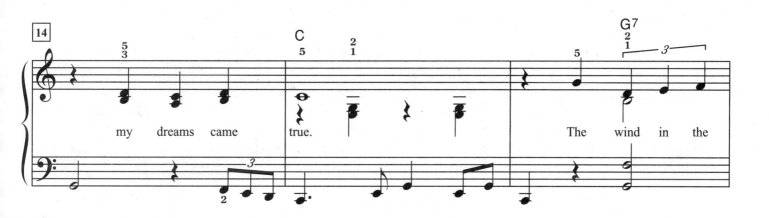

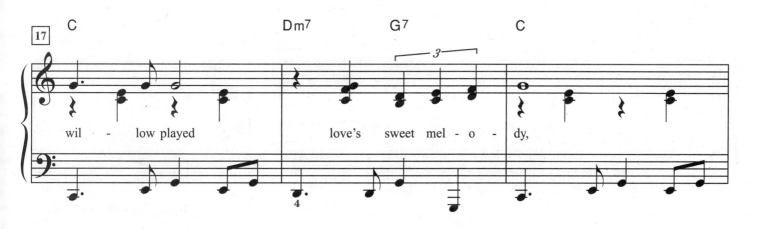

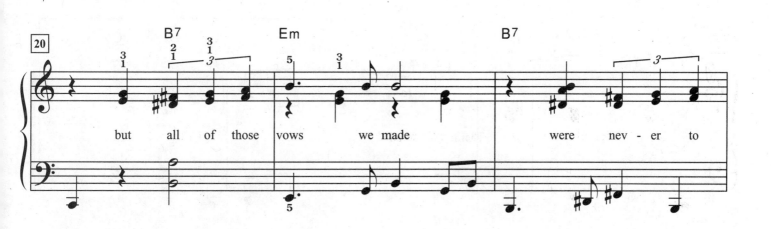

be. Though we're a - part, you're part of me

still for you were my thrill

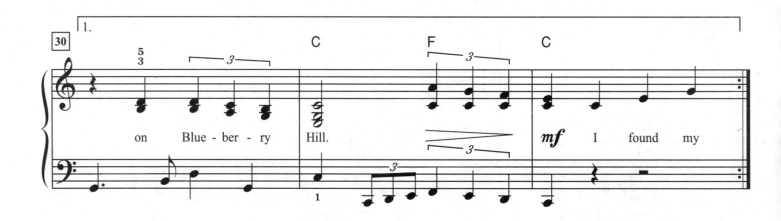

1.

on Blue - ber - ry Hill. mf I found my

2.

on Blue - ber - ry Hill. rit. e dim. mp

BORN TO RUN

Words and Music by Bruce Springsteen
Arranged by Dan Coates

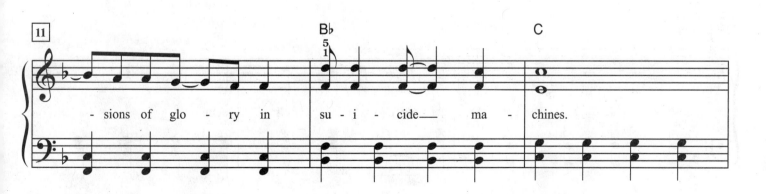

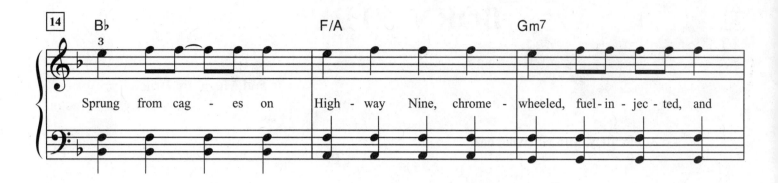

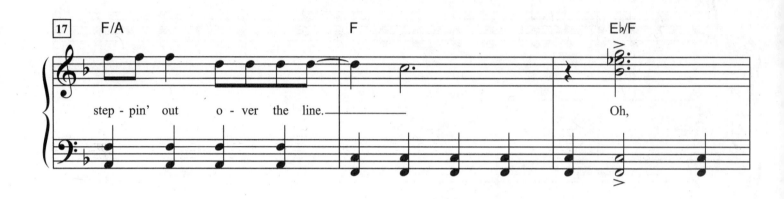

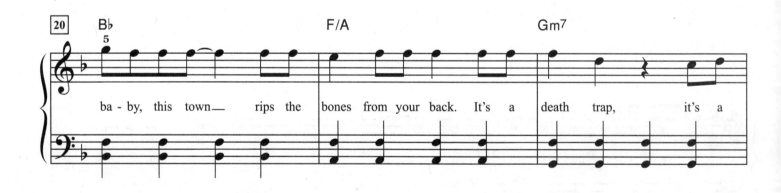

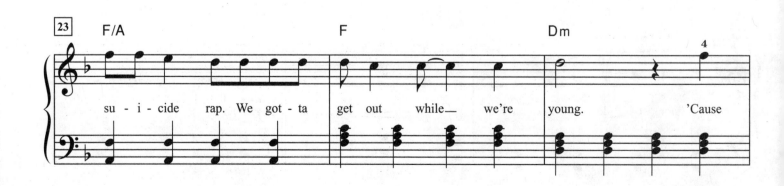

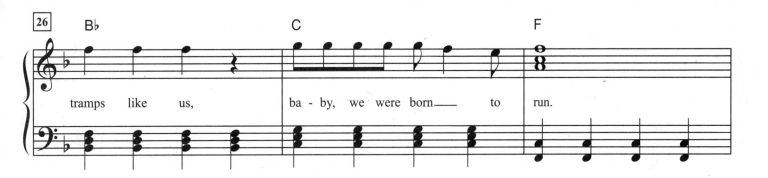

tramps like us, ba - by, we were born___ to run.

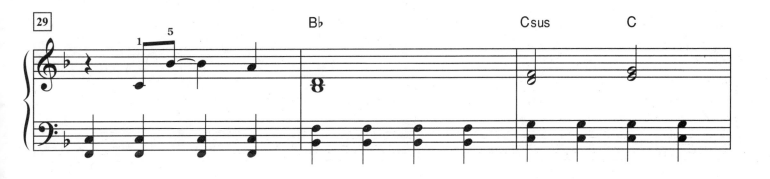

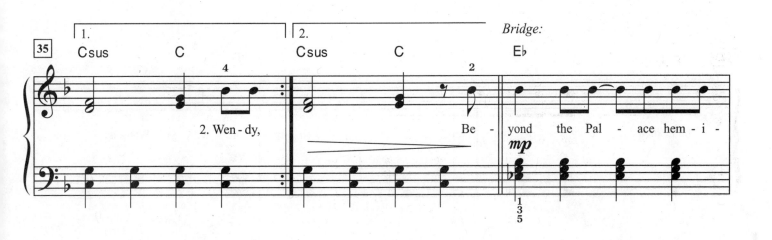

2. Wen - dy,

Be - yond the Pal - ace hem - i -

Bridge:

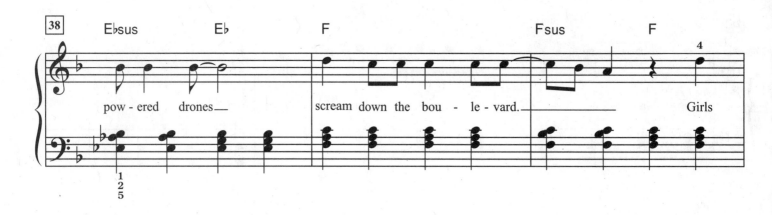

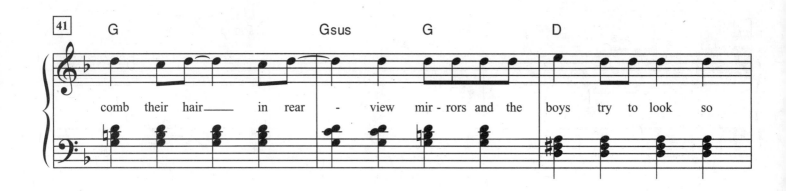

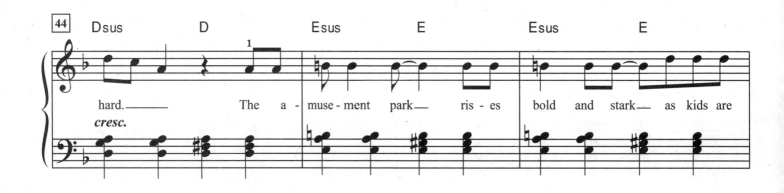

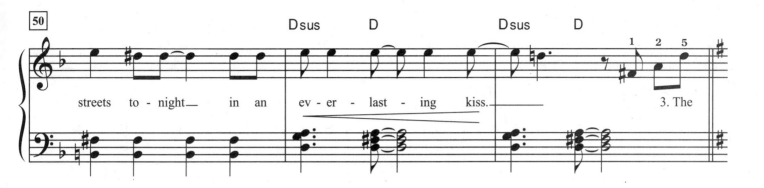

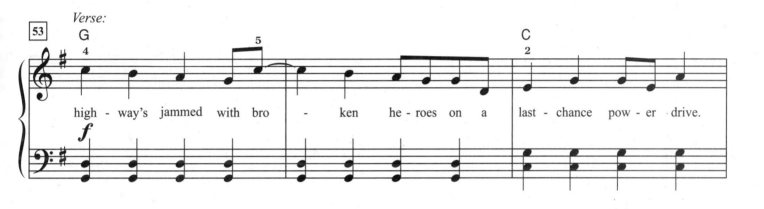

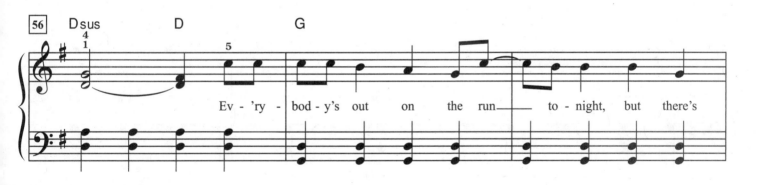

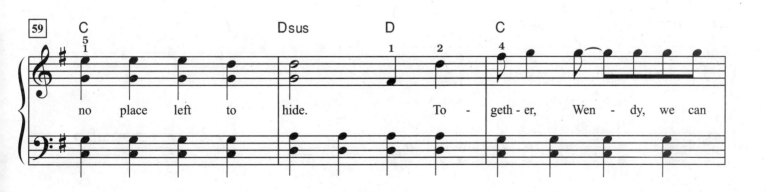

live with the sad - ness, I'll love you with all the mad - ness in my

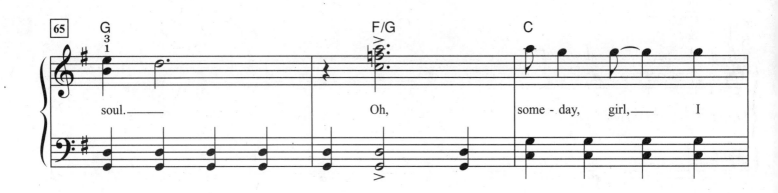

soul._____ Oh, some - day, girl,_____ I

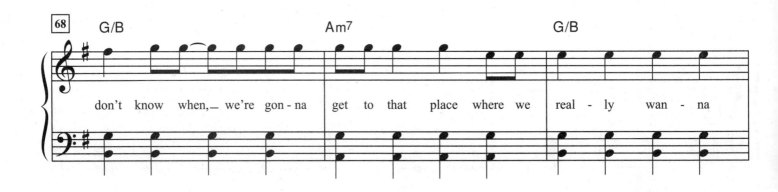

don't know when,— we're gon - na get to that place where we real - ly wan - na

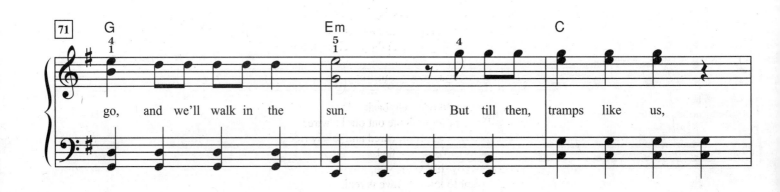

go, and we'll walk in the sun. But till then, tramps like us,

ba - by, we were born— to run.

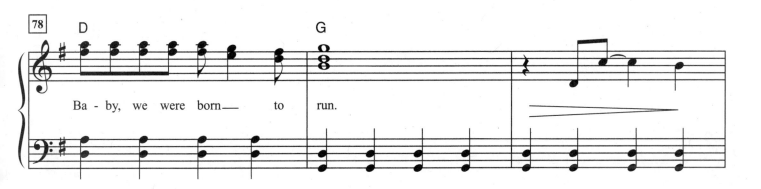

Ba - by, we were born— to run.

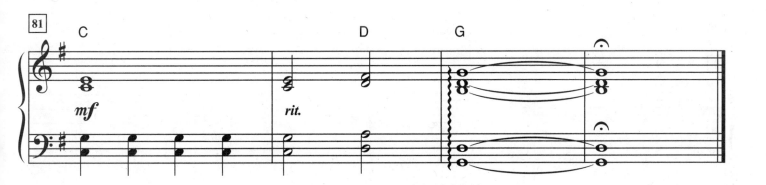

mf

rit.

Verse 2:
Wendy, let me in, I wanna be your friend,
I wanna guard your dreams and visions.
Just wrap your legs 'round these velvet rims,
And strap your hands 'cross my engines.
Together we could break this trap.
We'll run till we drop,
And, baby, we'll never go back.
Oh, will you walk with me out on the wire?
'Cause, baby, I'm just a scared and lonely rider,
But I got to know how it feels.
I want to know if love is wild,
Babe, I want to know if love is real.

THE BOXER

Words and Music by Paul Simon
Arranged by Dan Coates

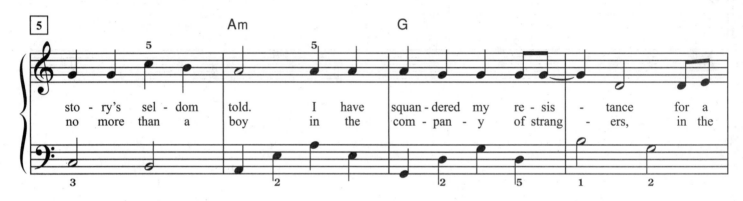

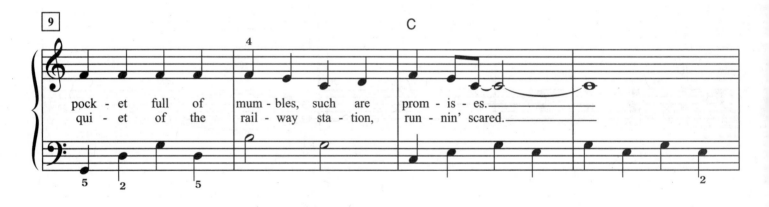

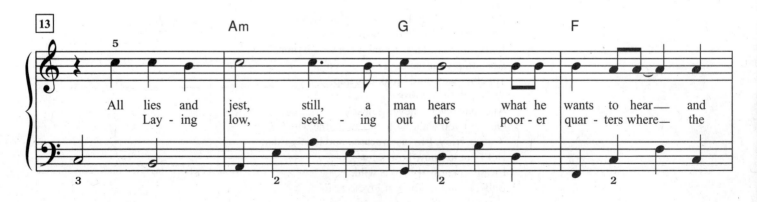

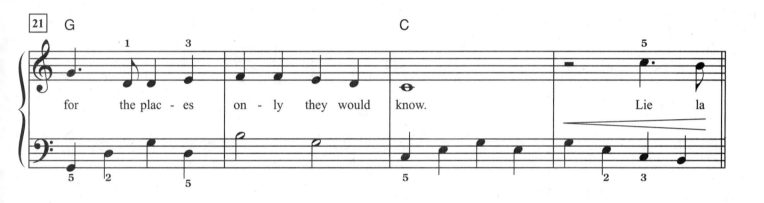

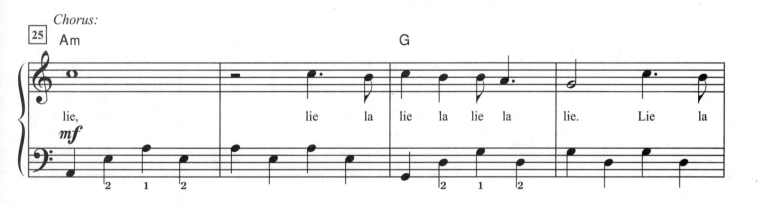

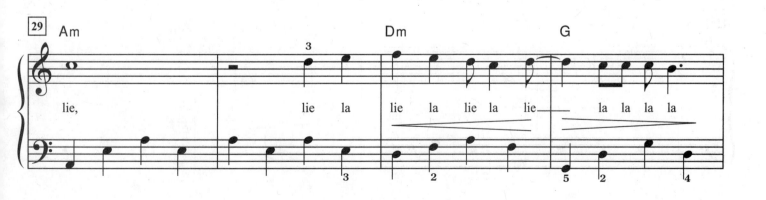

33 C

lie.———— dim. 3. Ask - ing

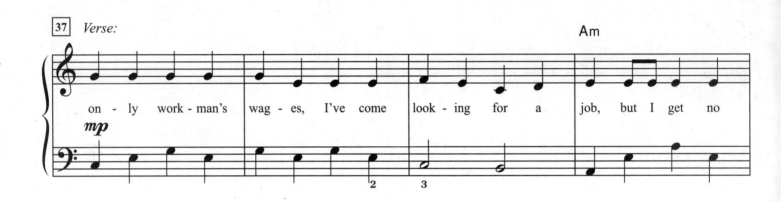

37 *Verse:* Am

on - ly work - man's wag - es, I've come look - ing for a job, but I get no

mp

41 G

of - fers,———— just a come - on from the whores on Sev - enth

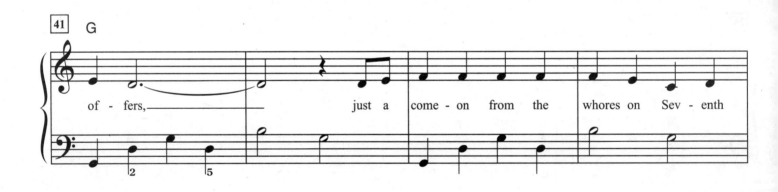

45 C Am

Av - e - nue.———— I do de - clare, there were

mf

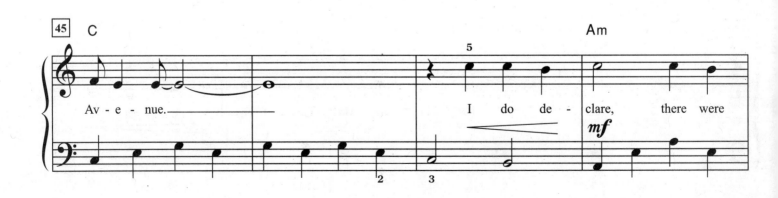

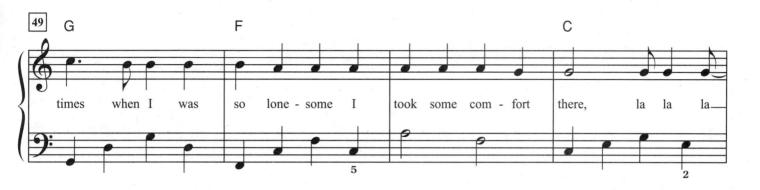

times when I was so lone - some I took some com - fort there, la la la___

___ la la la la.

4. Then I'm

Verse:

lay - ing out my win - ter clothes and wish - ing I was gone, go - in'

home,___ where the New York Cit - y win - ters are - n't

37

DESPERADO

Words and Music by
Don Henley and Glenn Frey
Arranged by Dan Coates

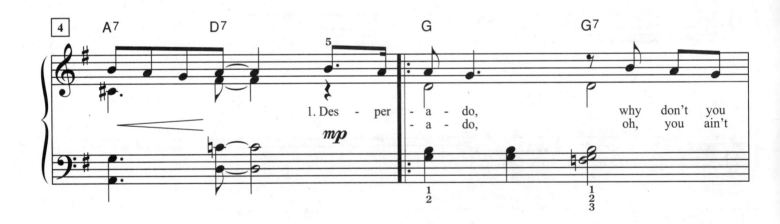

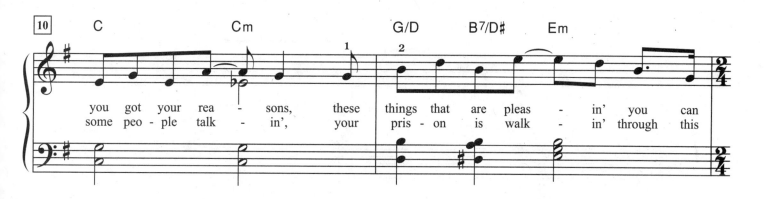

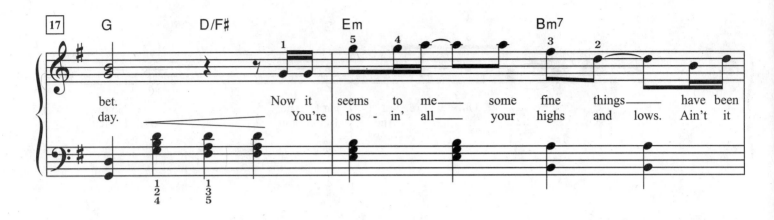

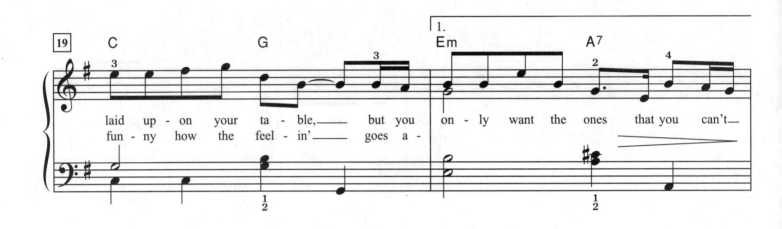

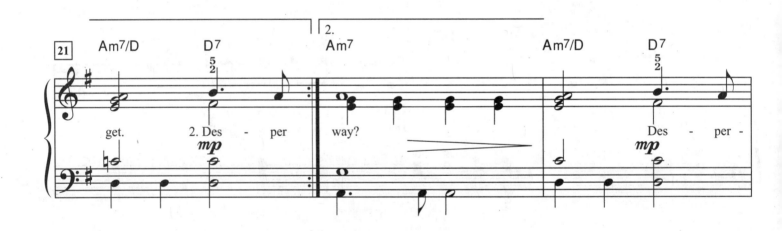

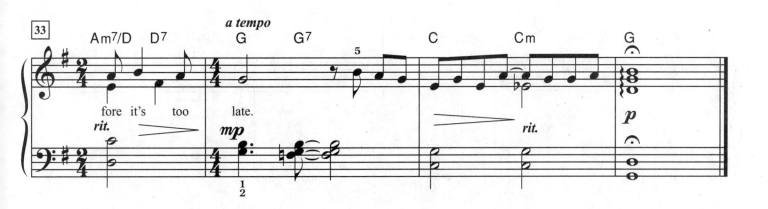

EARTH ANGEL
(WILL YOU BE MINE)

Words and Music by Jesse Belvin
Arranged by Dan Coates

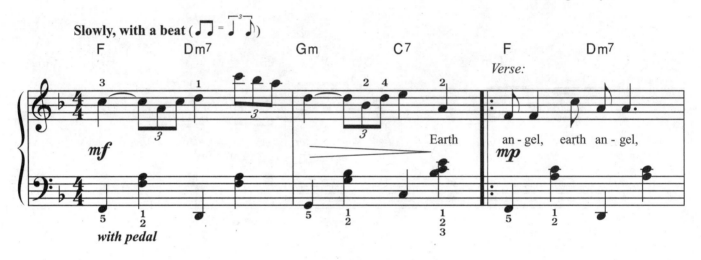

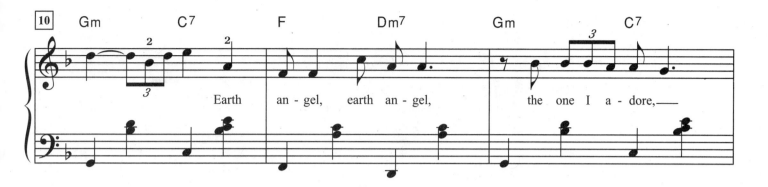

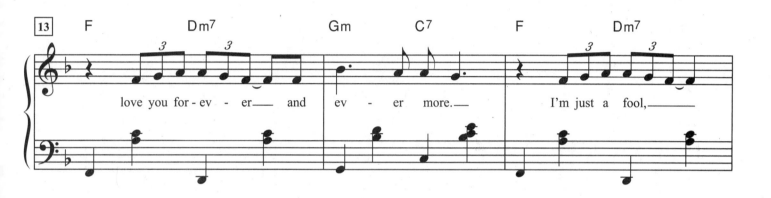

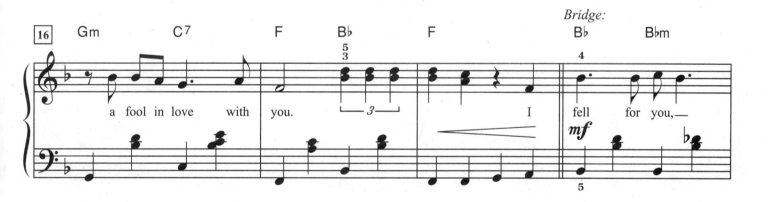

44

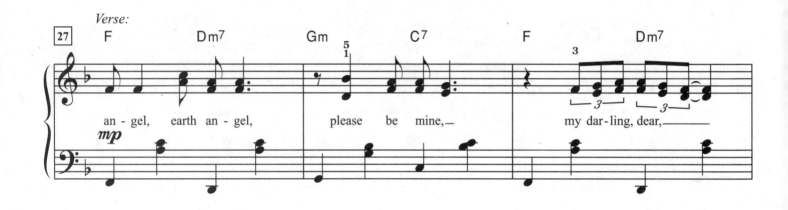

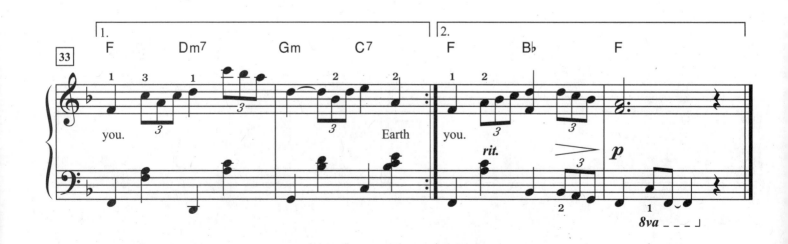

FAKE PLASTIC TREES

Words and Music by
Thomas Yorke, Edward O'Brien, Colin Greenwood,
Jonathan Greenwood and Philip Selway
Arranged by Dan Coates

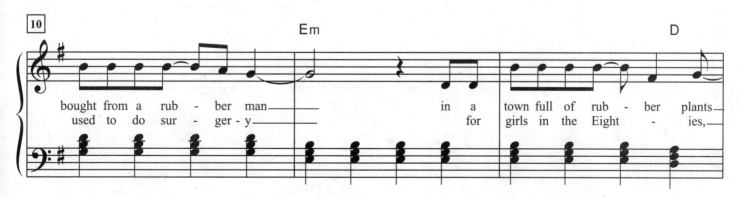

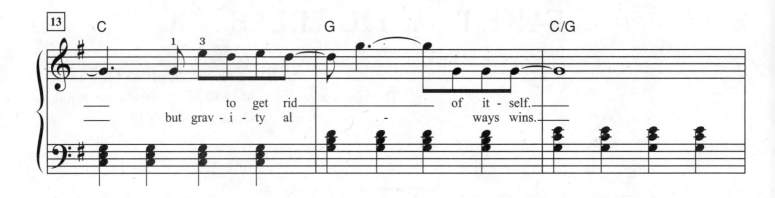

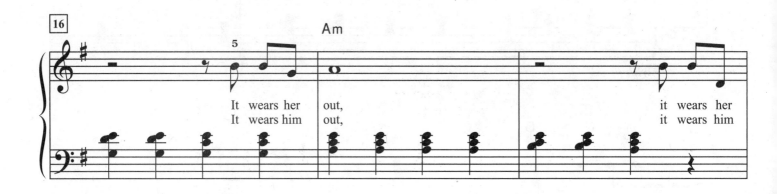

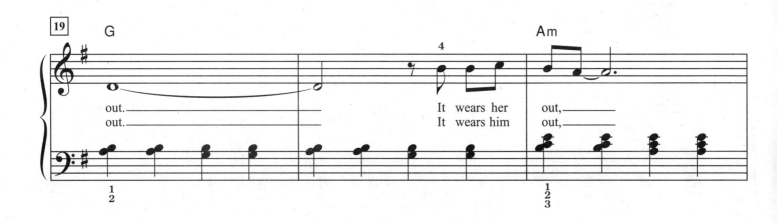

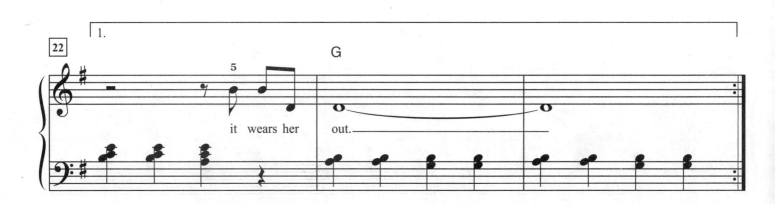

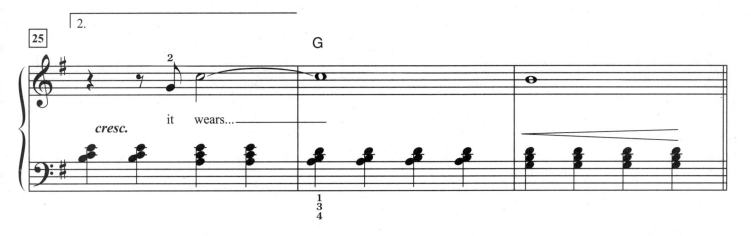

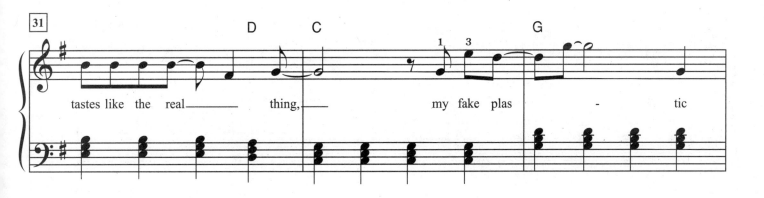

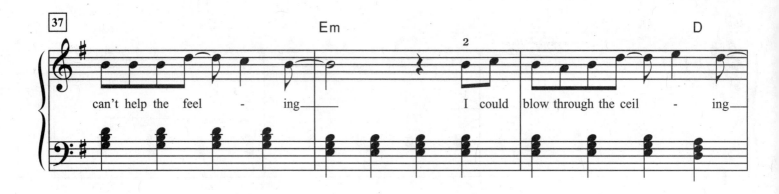

can't help the feel - ing___ I could blow through the ceil - ing___

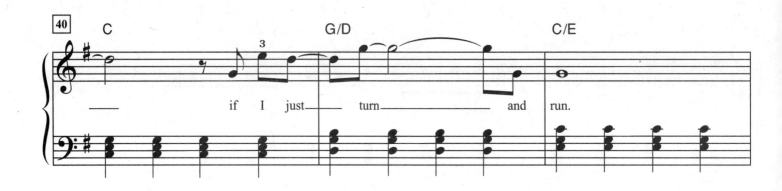

___ if I just___ turn___ and run.

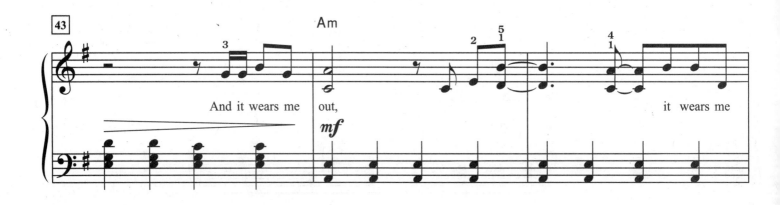

And it wears me out, it wears me

out. It wears me out,

49
G
it wears me out. And if I could be
52
Am
G
who you want - ed, if I could be who you want -
55
Am
- ed, all the time, all
58
G
Am
the time.
mp
61
G
rit.

GREAT BALLS OF FIRE

Words and Music by
Otis Blackwell and Jack Hammer
Arranged by Dan Coates

51

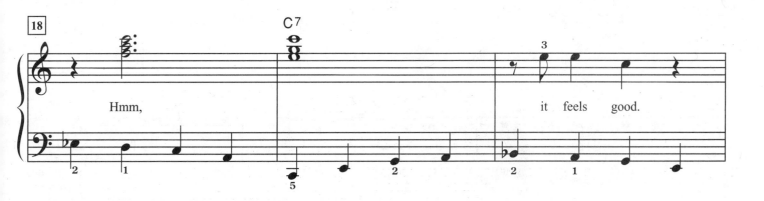

I CAN SEE FOR MILES

Words and Music by Peter Townshend
Arranged by Dan Coates

Moderately fast, with a steady beat

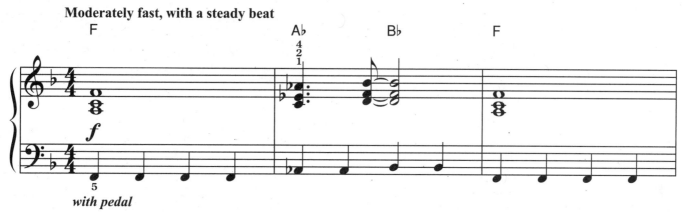

with pedal

Verse:

1. I know you've de-ceived me, now here's a sur-prise.

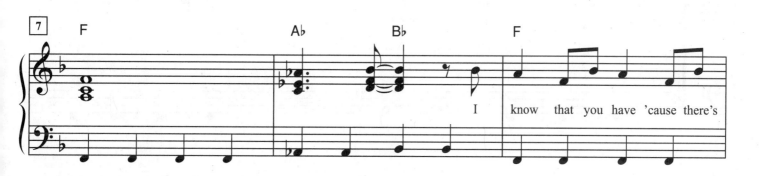

I know that you have 'cause there's

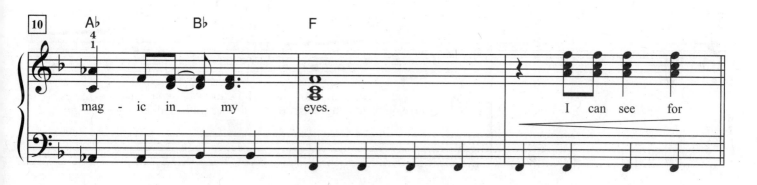

mag - ic in___ my eyes. I can see for

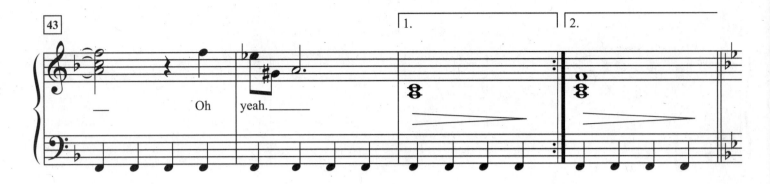

Oh yeah._____

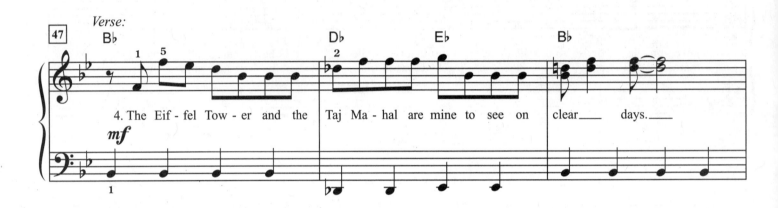

Verse:

4. The Eif - fel Tow - er and the Taj Ma - hal are mine to see on clear___ days.___

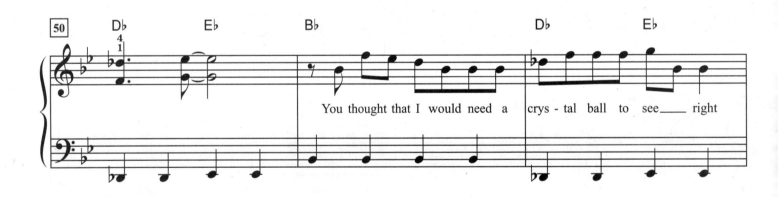

You thought that I would need a crys - tal ball to see___ right

through the haze.___ Well, here's a poke at you, you're gon - na

I GOT YOU BABE

Words and Music by Sonny Bono
Arranged by Dan Coates

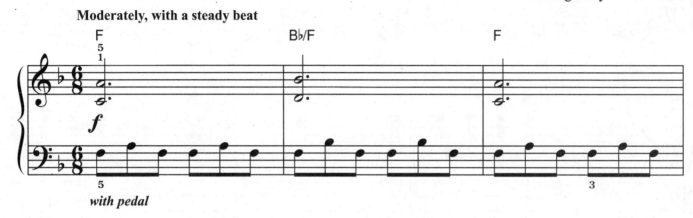

59

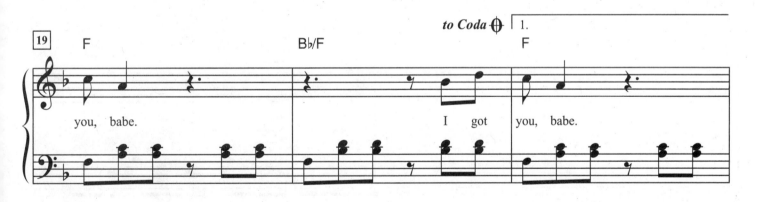

60

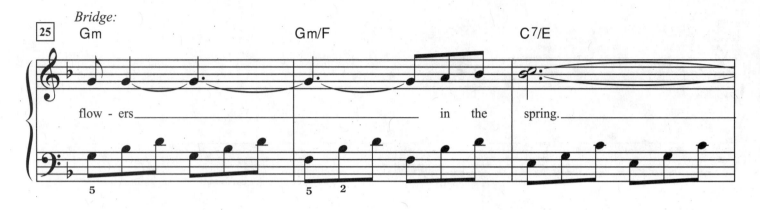

D.S. al Coda

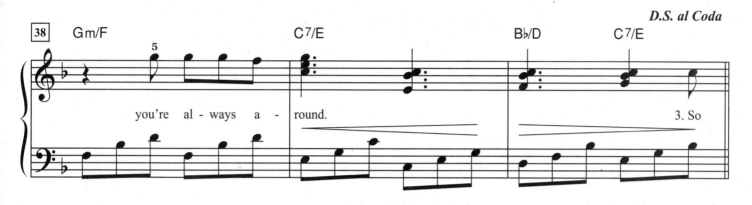

you're al - ways a - round.   3. So

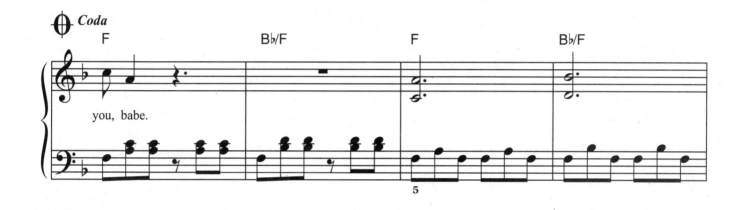

Coda

you, babe.

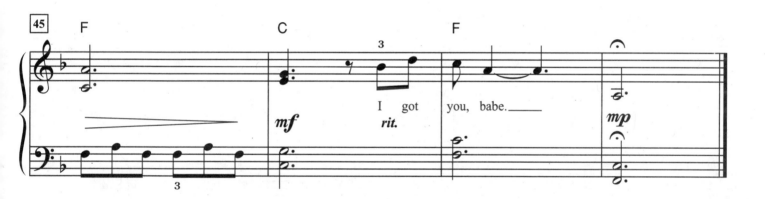

I got   you, babe._____

mf   *rit.*   *mp*

Verse 2:
They say our love won't pay the rent,
Before it's earned our money's all been spent.
I guess that's so, we don't have a pot,
But at least I'm sure of all the things we got.
(To Chorus:)

Verse 3:
So let them say your hair's too long,
'Cause I don't care, with you I can't be wrong.
Then put your little hand in mine,
There ain't no hill or mountain we can't climb.
(To Chorus:)

I WANNA BE SEDATED

Words and Music by
Jeffrey Hyman, John Cummings and Douglas Colvin
Arranged by Dan Coates

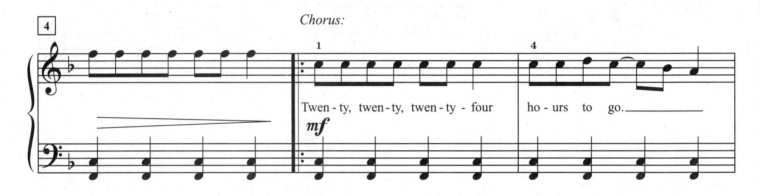

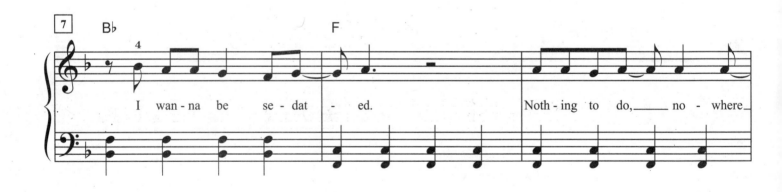

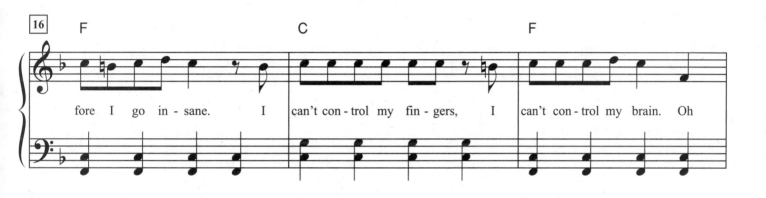

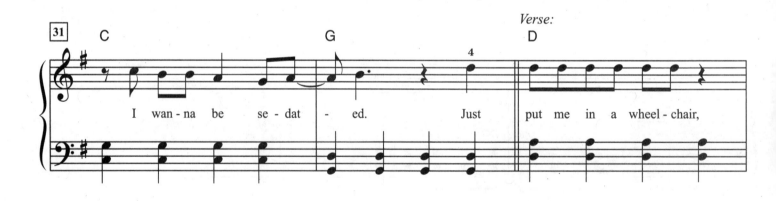

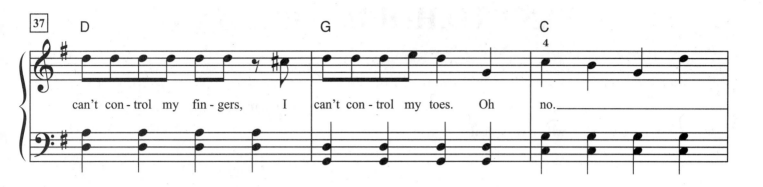

can't con-trol my fin-gers, I can't con-trol my toes. Oh no._____

(play 3 times)

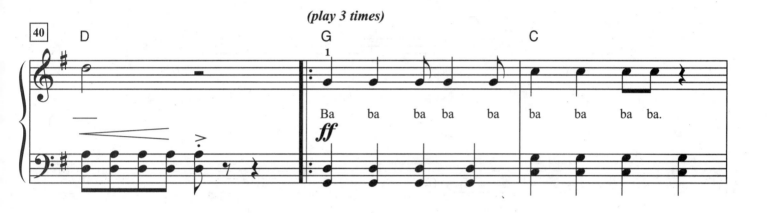

Ba ba ba ba ba ba ba ba ba.

ff

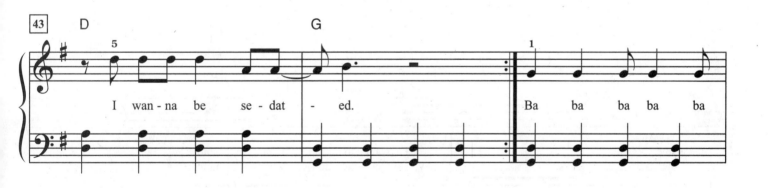

I wan-na be se-dat - ed. Ba ba ba ba ba

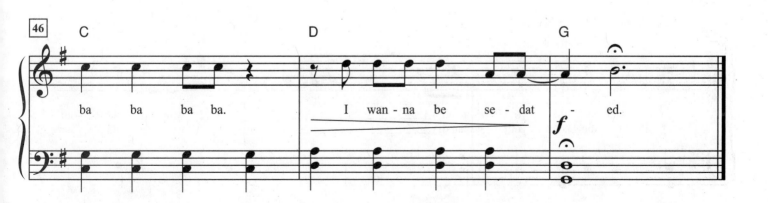

ba ba ba ba. I wan-na be se-dat - ed.

f

I WANT TO HOLD YOUR HAND

Words and Music by
John Lennon and Paul McCartney
Arranged by Dan Coates

Moderately, with a rock beat

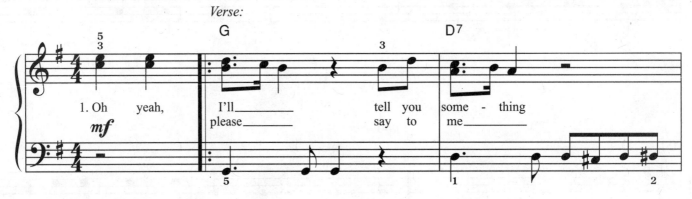

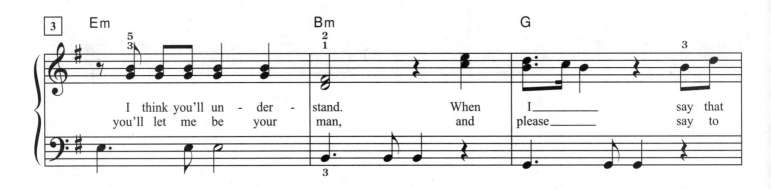

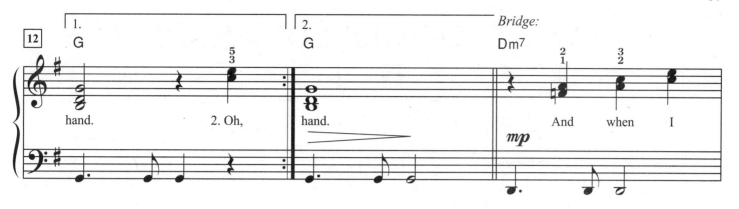

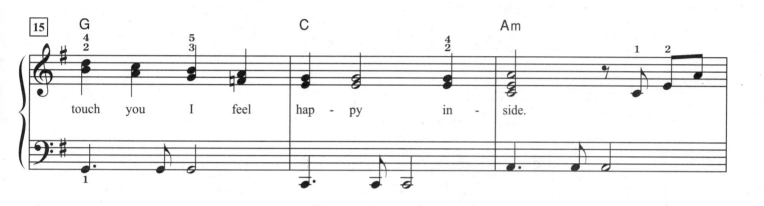

LIKE A ROLLING STONE

Words and Music by Bob Dylan
Arranged by Dan Coates

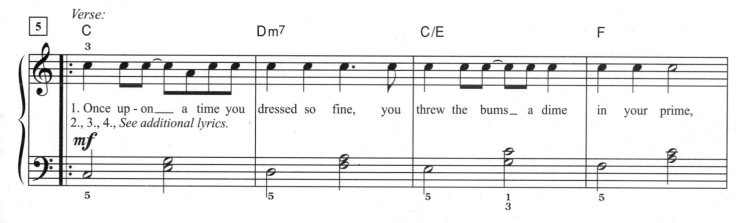

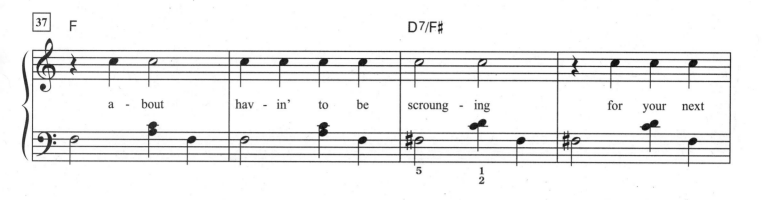
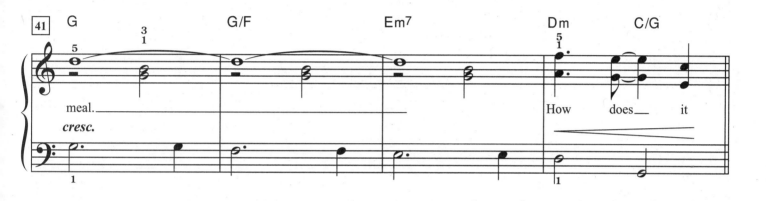

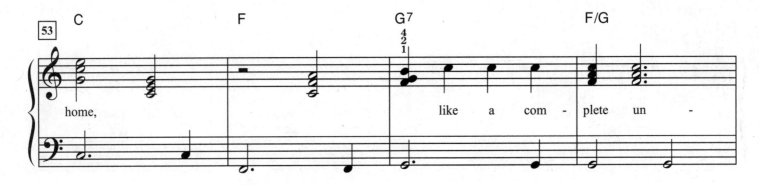

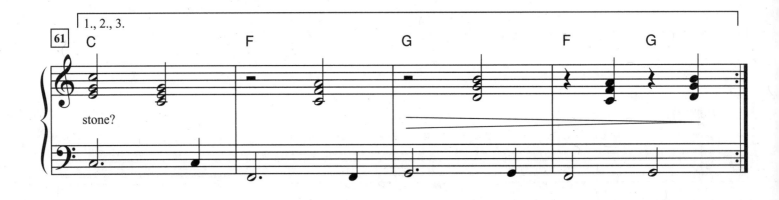

Verse 2:
Oh, you've gone to the finest school, alright, Miss Lonely,
But you know you only used to get juiced in it.
Nobody's ever taught you how to live out on the street
And now you're gonna have to get used to it.
You say you never compromise
With the mystery tramp, but now you realize
He's not selling any alibis
As you stare into the vacuum of his eyes
And say, "Do you want to make a deal?"
(To Chorus:)

Verse 3:
Oh, you never turned around to see the frowns on the jugglers and the clowns
When they all did tricks for you?
Never understood that it ain't no good,
You shouldn't let other people get your kicks for you.
You used to ride on a chrome horse with your diplomat
Who carried on his shoulder a Siamese cat.
Ain't it hard when you discovered that
He really wasn't where it's at
After he took from you everything he could steal?
(To Chorus:)

Verse 4:
Princess on the steeple and all the pretty people,
They're all drinkin', thinkin' that they got it made.
Exchanging all precious gifts,
But you better take your diamond ring,
You'd better pawn it, babe.
You used to be so amused
At Napoleon in rags and the language that he used.
Go to him now, he calls you, you can't refuse.
When you got nothin', you got nothin' to lose.
You're invisible now, you got no secrets to conceal.
(To Chorus:)

IN MY ROOM

Words and Music by
Brian Wilson and Gary Usher
Arranged by Dan Coates

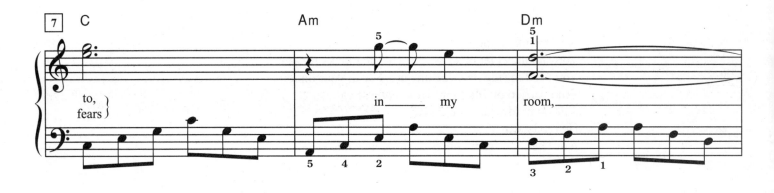

KNOCKING ON HEAVEN'S DOOR

Words and Music by Bob Dylan
Arranged by Dan Coates

Moderately slow
Verse:

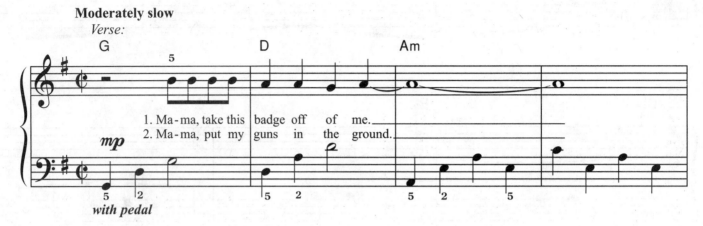

1. Ma - ma, take this badge off of me.
2. Ma - ma, put my guns in the ground.

with pedal

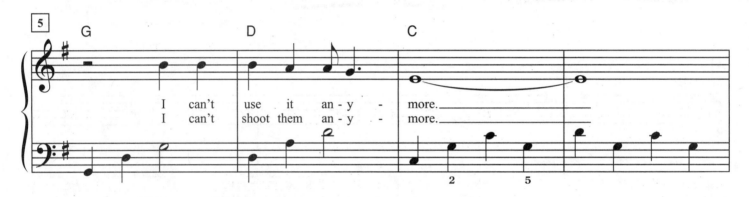

I can't use it an - y - more.
I can't shoot them an - y - more.

It's get - tin' dark,___ too dark___ to see.___
That long, black cloud___ is com - in' down.___

I feel like I'm knock - in' on Hea - ven's door.___
I feel like I'm knock - in' on Hea - ven's door.___

LOVE ME TENDER

Words by Elvis Presley and Vera Matson
Music traditional (*Aura Lee*—American folk song)
Arranged by Dan Coates

all my dreams ful - fill. For, my dar - lin',

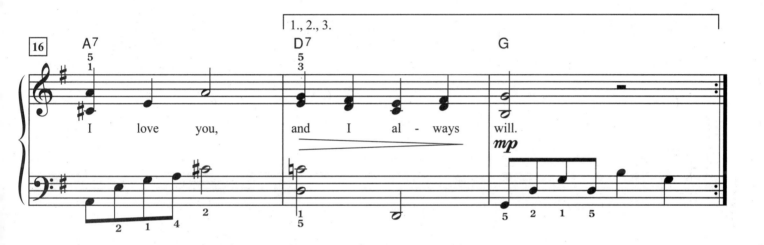

1., 2., 3.

I love you, and I al - ways will.

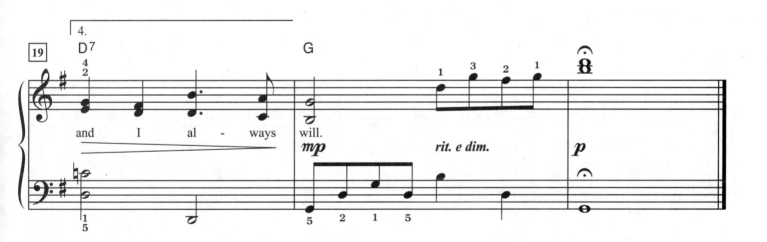

4.

and I al - ways will.

Verse 2:
Love me tender, love me long,
Take me to your heart.
For it's there that I belong,
And we'll never part.
(To Chorus:)

Verse 3:
Love me tender, love me dear,
Tell me you are mine.
I'll be yours through all the years
Till the end of time.
(To Chorus:)

Verse 4:
When at last my dreams come true,
Darling, this I know:
Happiness will follow you
Everywhere you go:
(To Chorus:)

MAGGIE MAY

Words and Music by
Rod Stewart and Martin Quittenton
Arranged by Dan Coates

Moderately, with a steady beat

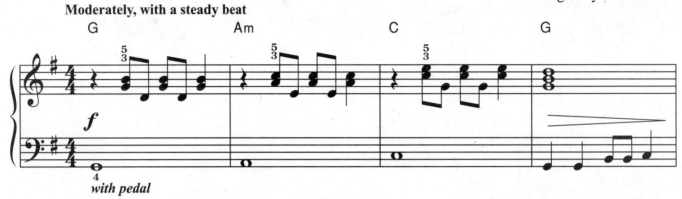

Wake up, Mag-gie, I think I got some-thing to say to you.— It's

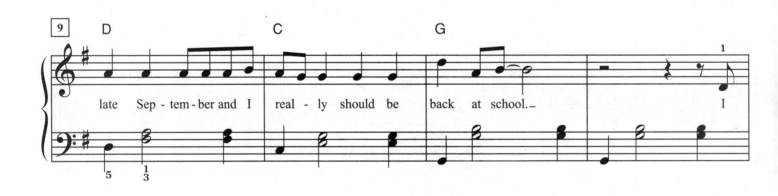

late Sep-tem-ber and I real-ly should be back at school.— I

know I keep you a-mused,— but I feel I'm be-ing used. Oh,

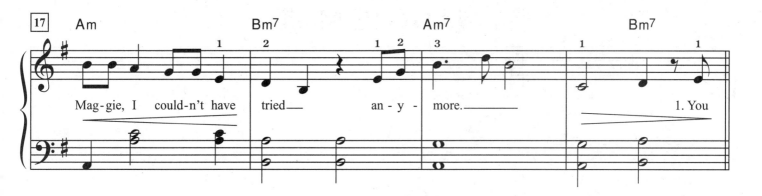

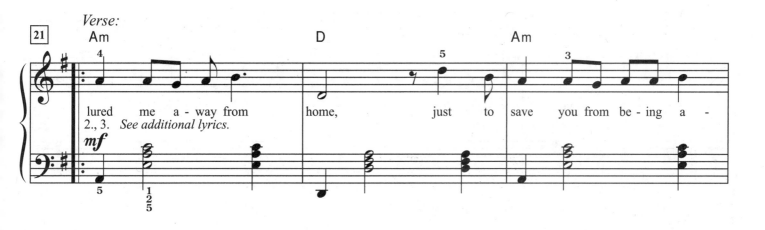

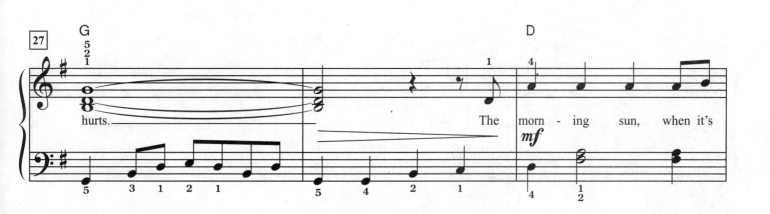

in your face, real-ly shows your age, — but that don't wor-ry me

none, in my eyes you're ev-'ry-thing. — I laughed at all of your

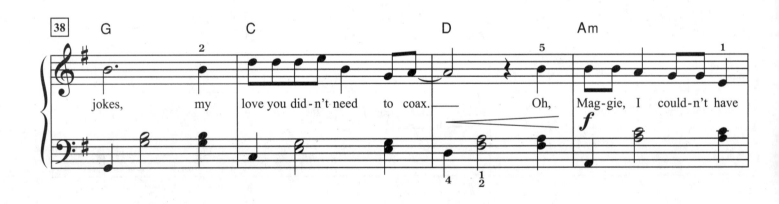

jokes, my love you did-n't need to coax. — Oh, Mag-gie, I could-n't have

tried — an-y more. —
2. You
3. You

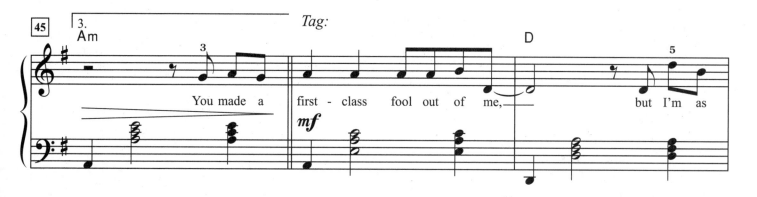

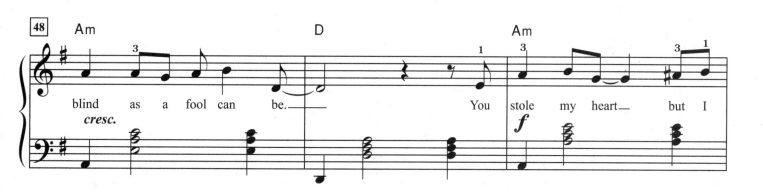

Verse 2:
You lured me away from home, just to save you from being alone.
You stole my soul, that's a pain I can do without.
All I needed was a friend to lend a guiding hand.
But you turned into a lover, and Mother, what a lover! You wore me out.
All you did was wreck my bed, and in the morning kick me in the head.
Oh, Maggie, I couldn't have tried anymore.

Verse 3:
You lured me away from home, 'cause you didn't want to be alone.
You stole my heart, I couldn't leave you if I tried.
I suppose I could collect my books and get back to school.
Or steal my Daddy's cue and make a living out of playin' pool,
Or find myself a rock and roll band that needs a helpin' hand.
Oh, Maggie, I wish I'd never seen your face.
(To Tag:)

O-O-H CHILD

Words and Music by Stan Vincent
Arranged by Dan Coates

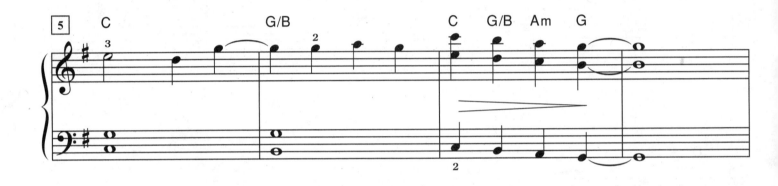

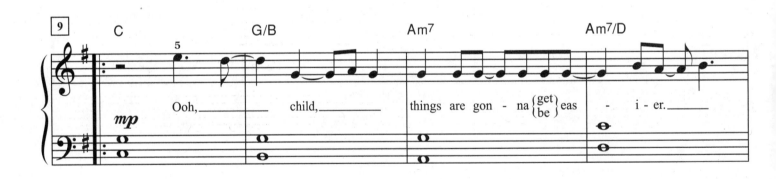

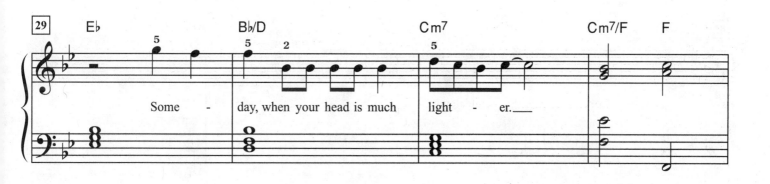

Some - day, yeah,__ we'll walk in the rays of a beau-ti-ful sun.____

Some - day, when the world is much bright - er.____

La - la - la - la - la - la - la - la - la.____

La - la - la - la - la - la - la - la.

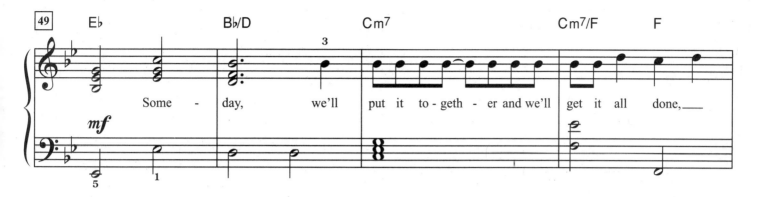

Some - day, we'll put it to - geth - er and we'll get it all done,___

some - day, when your head is much light - er.___

Some - day, we'll walk in the rays of a beau - ti - ful sun,___

some - day, when the world is much bright - er.___ Right

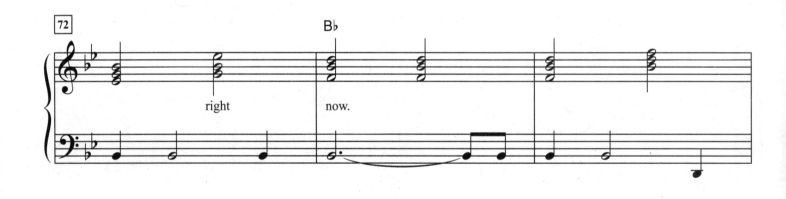

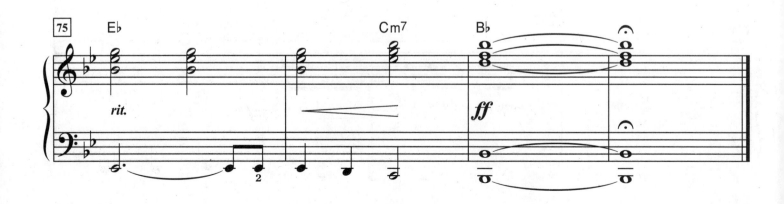

PAINT IT, BLACK

Words and Music by
Mick Jagger and Keith Richards
Arranged by Dan Coates

Moderately, with a steady beat

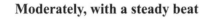

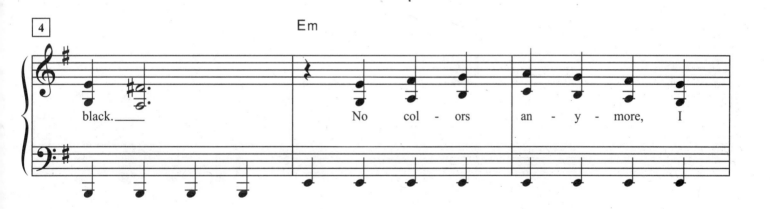

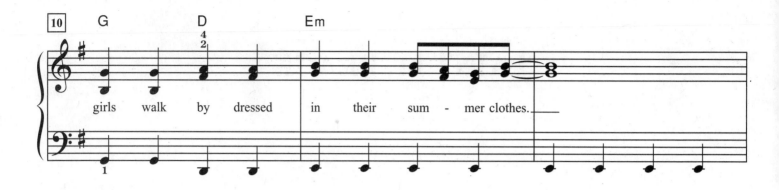

girls walk by dressed in their sum - mer clothes.

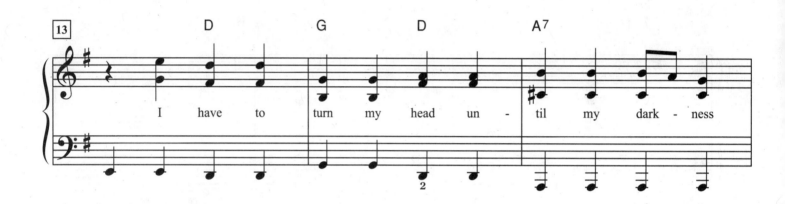

I have to turn my head un - til my dark - ness

1., 2., 3., 4.   5.

goes.   goes.   Mm.

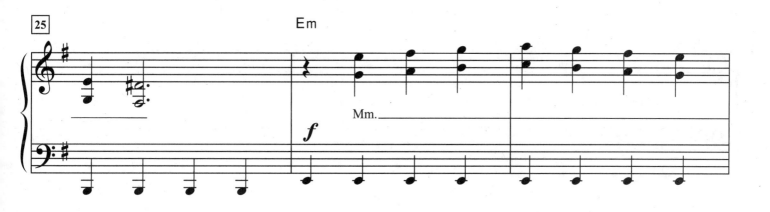

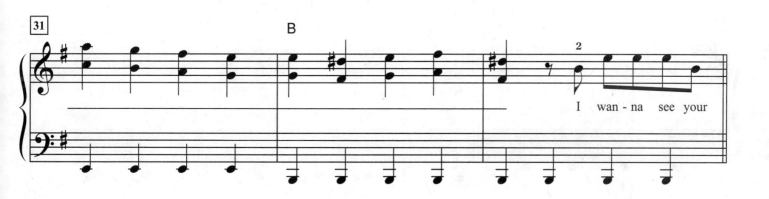

I wan - na see your

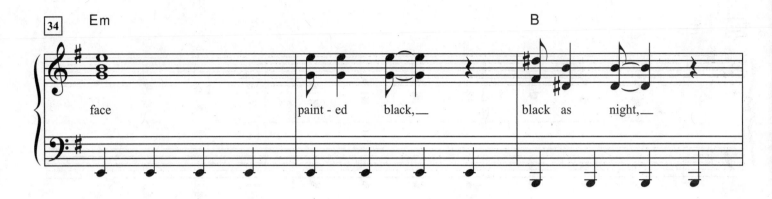

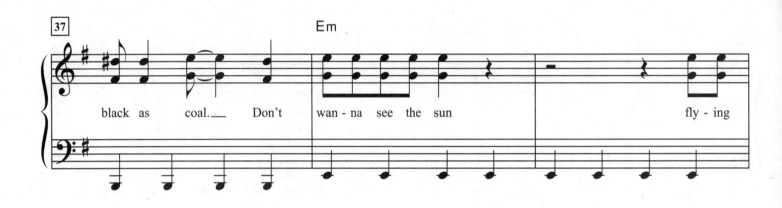

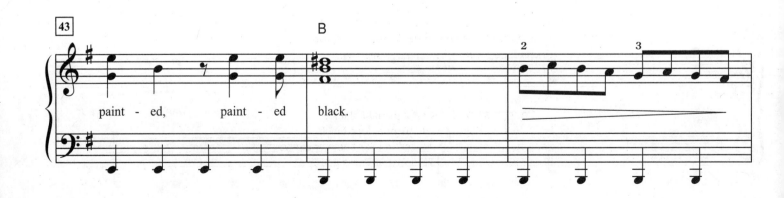

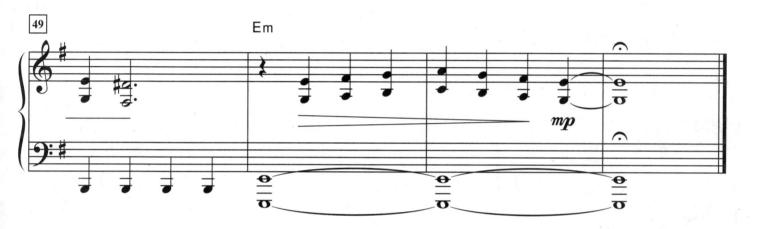

Verse 2:
I see a line of cars and they're all painted black,
With flowers and my love both never to come back.
I see people turn their heads and quickly look away,
Like a newborn baby, it just happens ev'ry day.

Verse 3:
I look inside myself and see my heart is black.
I see my red door, I must have it painted black.
Maybe then I'll fade away and not have to face the facts.
It's not easy facing up when your whole world is black.

Verse 4:
No more will my green sea go turn a deeper blue.
I could not foresee this thing happening to you.
If I look hard enough into the setting sun,
My love will laugh with me before the mornin' comes.

Verse 5:
I see a red door, and I want it painted black.
No colors anymore, I want them to turn black.
I see the girls walk by dressed in their summer clothes.
I have to turn my head until my darkness goes.

PEOPLE GET READY

Words and Music by Curtis Mayfield
Arranged by Dan Coates

SAVE THE LAST DANCE FOR ME

Words and Music by
Mort Shuman and Doc Pomus
Arranged by Dan Coates

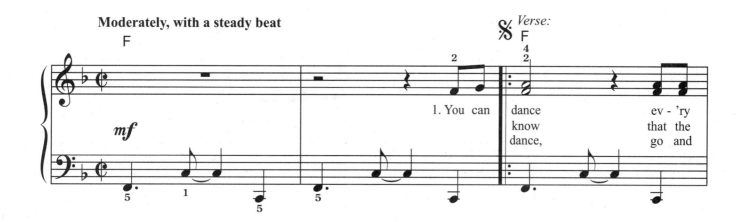

your hand ___ 'neath the pale moon - light. ___
your heart ___ to an - y - one. ___
take you home, you must tell him no. ___

But don't for -

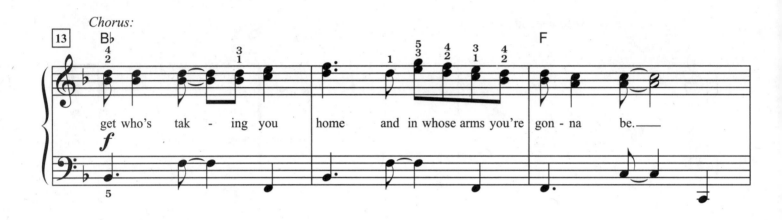

Chorus:

get who's tak - ing you home and in whose arms you're gon - na be. ___

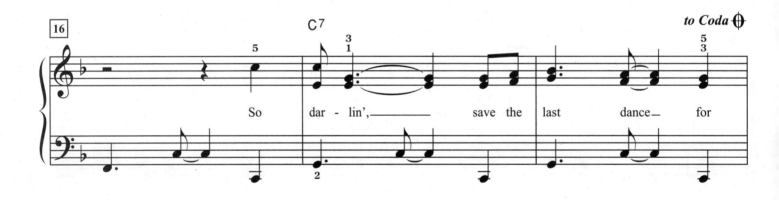

to Coda ⊕

So dar - lin', ___ save the last dance ___ for

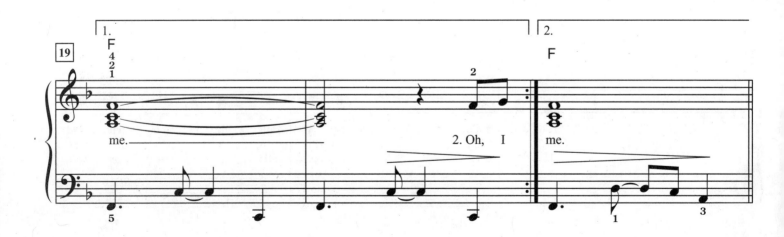

1.

me. ___   2. Oh, I

2.

me.

(WE'RE GONNA) ROCK AROUND THE CLOCK

Words and Music by
Max C. Freedman and Jimmy DeKnight
Arranged by Dan Coates

Moderately fast, with a steady rock beat

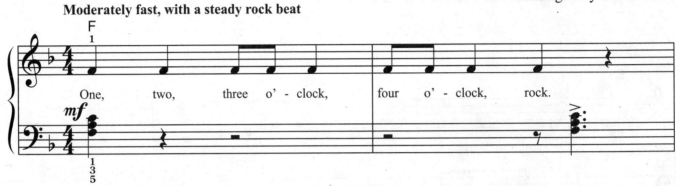

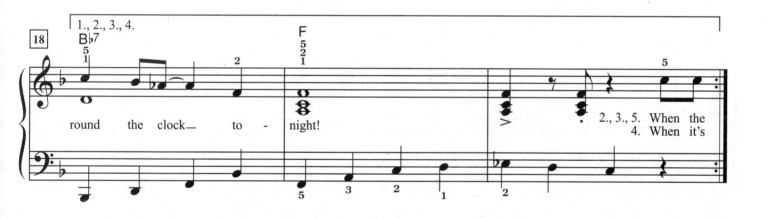

SAIL AWAY

Words and Music by Randy Newman
Arranged by Dan Coates

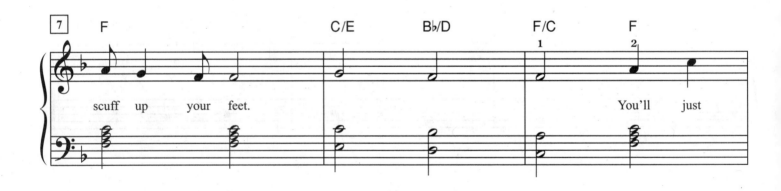

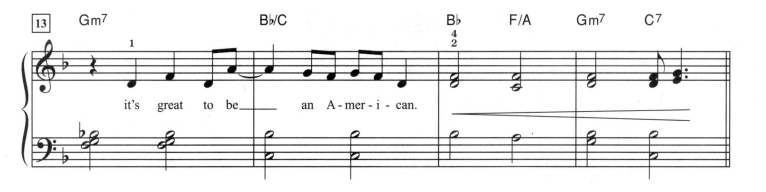

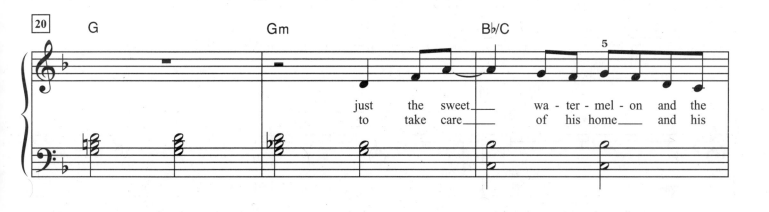

106

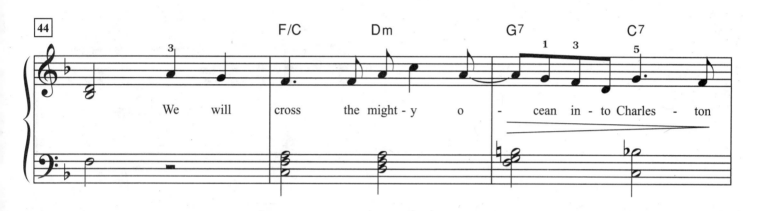

SH-BOOM

Words and Music by
James Keyes, Carl Feaster, Floyd McRae,
Claude Feaster and James Edwards
Arranged by Dan Coates

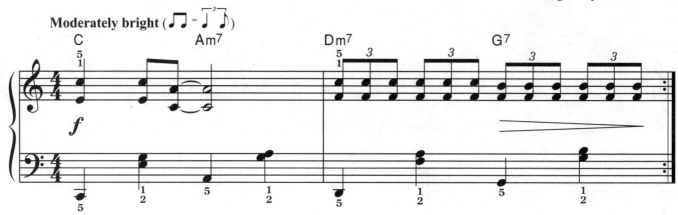

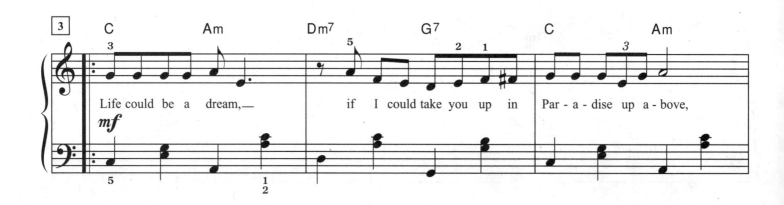

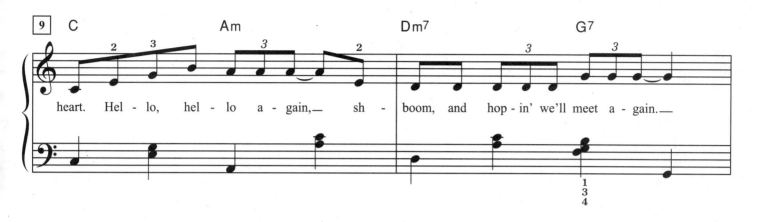

9 | C . . . . Am . . . . Dm7 . . . . G7

heart. Hel - lo, hel - lo a - gain,— sh - boom, and hop - in' we'll meet a - gain.—

11 | C . . . . Am . . . . Dm7 . . . . G7 . . . . C . . . . Am

Life could be a dream,— if on - ly all my pre-cious plans would come true,

14 | Dm7 . . . . G7 . . . . C . . . . Am . . . . Dm7 . . . . G7

if you would let me spend my whole life— lov - in' you, life could be a dream, sweet -

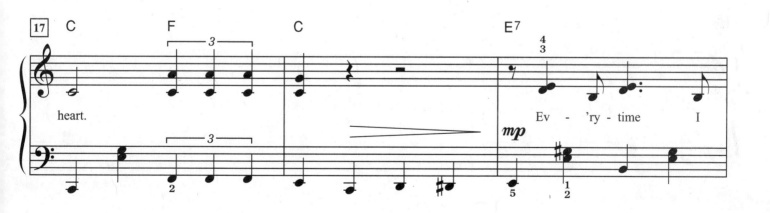

17 | C . . . . F . . . . C E7

heart. Ev - 'ry - time I

mp

look at you,— some - thing is on my mind.

If you'd do what I want you to,— ba - by, we'd be so

fine. Oh, life could be a dream,— if I could take you up in

Par - a - dise up a - bove, if you would tell me I'm the on - ly one that you love,

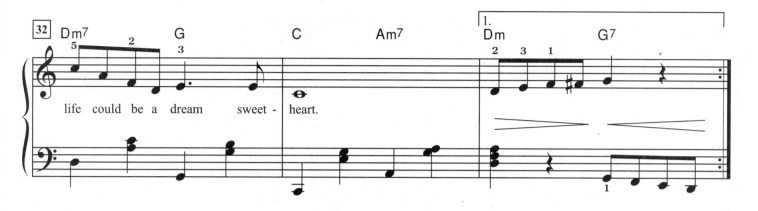

life could be a dream sweet - heart.

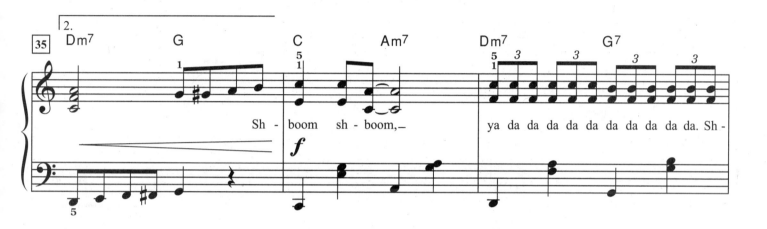

Sh - boom sh - boom,— ya da da da da da da da da da da. Sh -

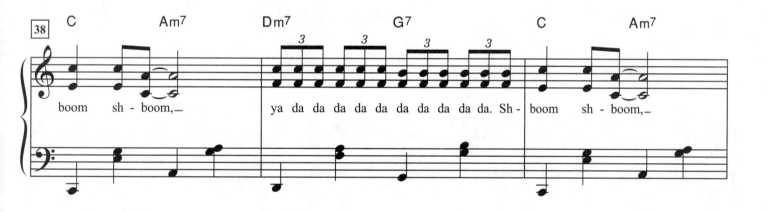

boom sh - boom,— ya da da da da da da da da da da. Sh - boom sh - boom,—

ya da da da da da da da da da da. Sh - boom.

THE SOUND OF SILENCE

Words and Music by Paul Simon
Arranged by Dan Coates

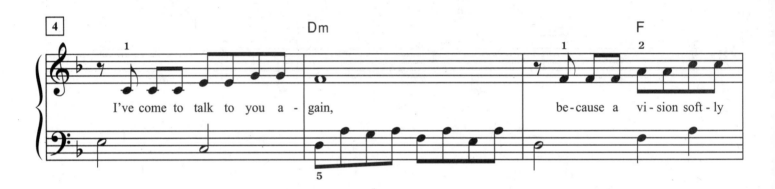

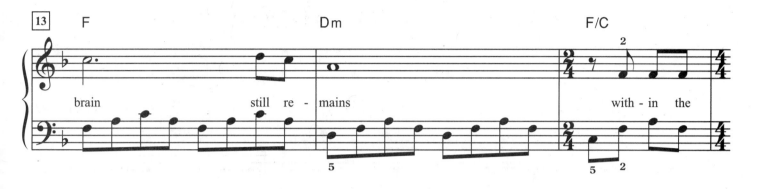

brain   still re - mains   with - in the

sound   of   si - lence._____   2. In rest-less dreams I walked a -
3. And in the nak - ed light I

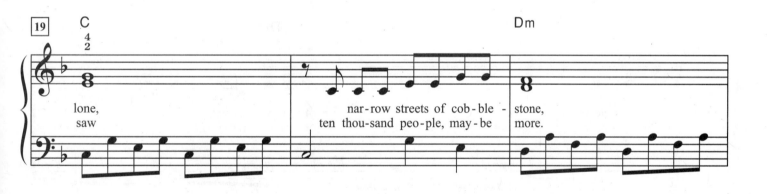

lone,
saw   nar-row streets of cob-ble - stone,
                                 ten thou-sand peo-ple, may-be more.

'neath the ha - lo of a   street   lamp,___   I turned my col - lar to the
Peo - ple talk - ing with-out speak   - ing,___   peo - ple hear-ing with-out

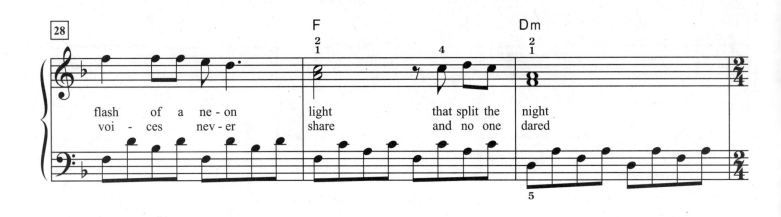

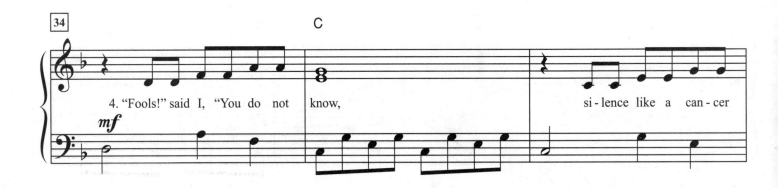

STAIRWAY TO HEAVEN

Words and Music by
Jimmy Page and Robert Plant
Arranged by Dan Coates

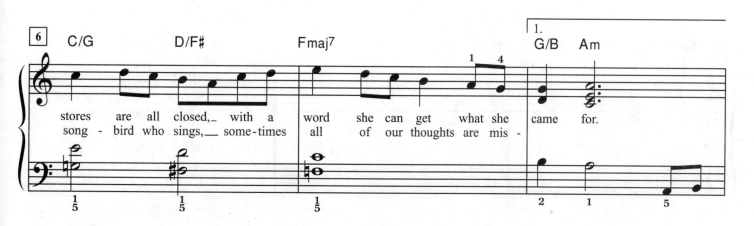

118

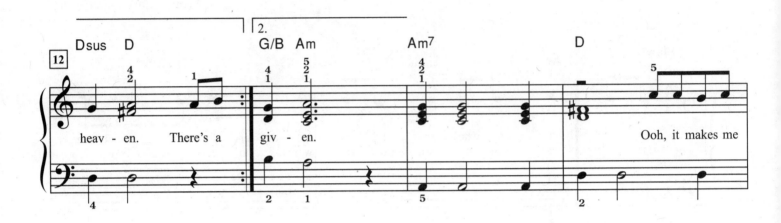

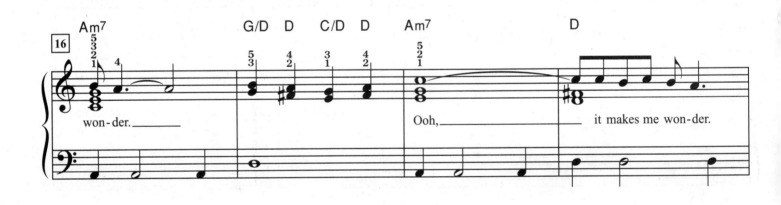

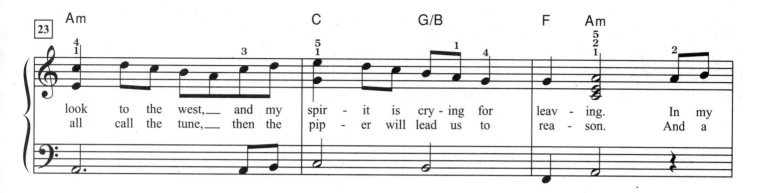

look to the west,___ and my spir - it is cry - ing for leav - ing. In my
all call the tune,___ then the pip - er will lead us to rea - son. And a

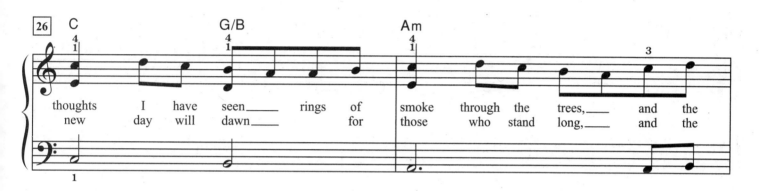

thoughts I have seen___ rings of smoke through the trees,___ and the
new day will dawn___ for those who stand long,___ and the

1.
2.

voic - es of those who stand look - ing. And it's laugh - ter.
for - ests will ech - o with

With a strong beat

If there's a bus - tle in your hedge - row,___ don't be a-larmed now,
Your head is hum - ming and it won't go,___ in case you don't know,

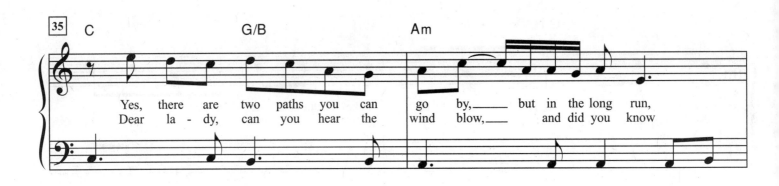

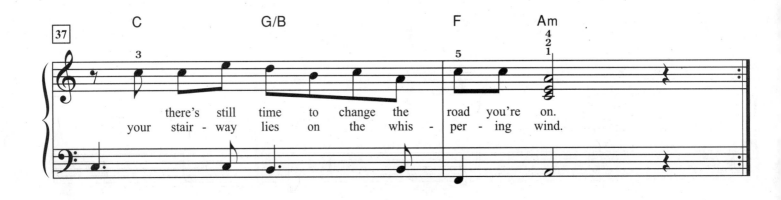

soul.___ / hard,___

There walks a la-dy we all know,___
the tune will come to you at last,___

who shines white light and wants to show___
when all are one and one is all,___

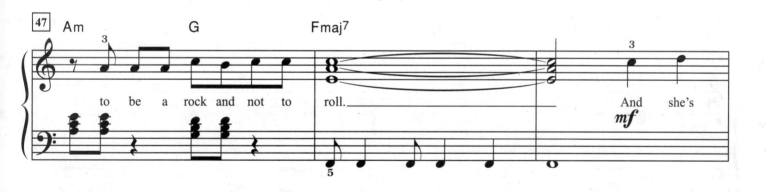

to be a rock and not to roll.___ And she's

buy- ing a stair- way to heav- en.___

STAND BY ME

Words and Music by
Jerry Leiber, Mike Stoller and Ben E. King
Arranged by Dan Coates

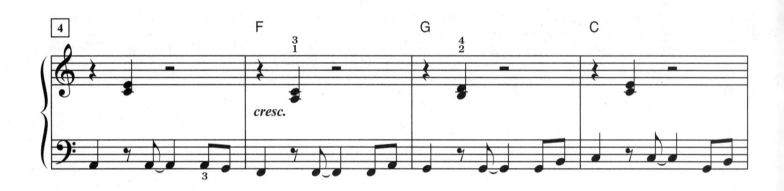

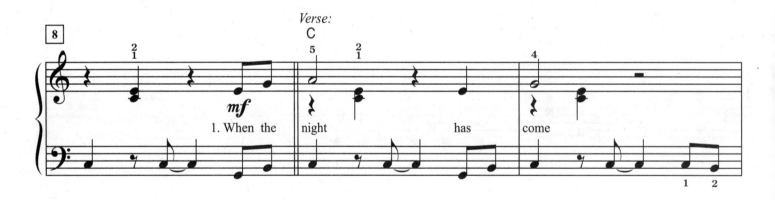

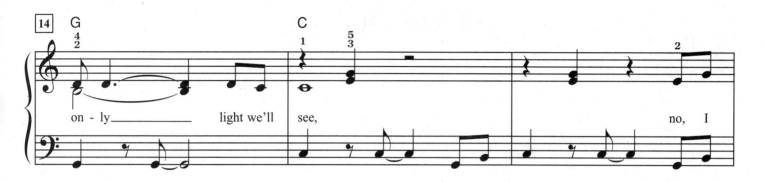

124

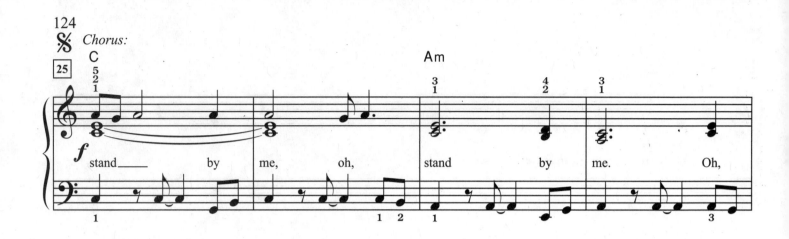

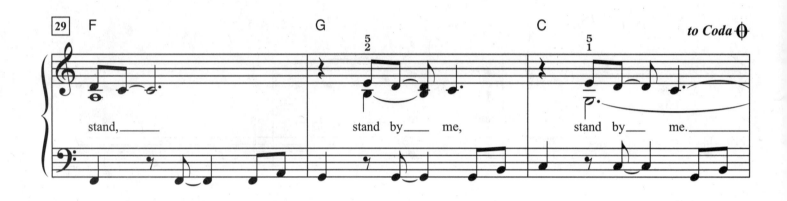

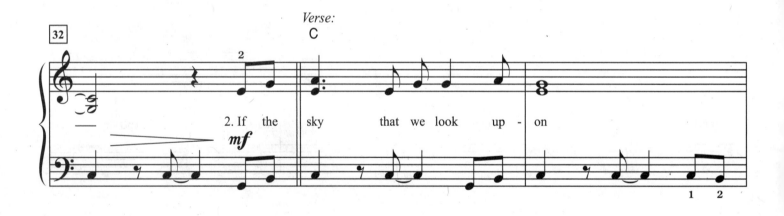

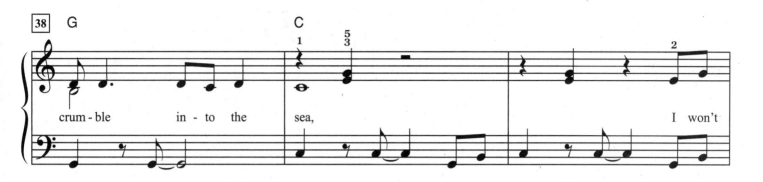

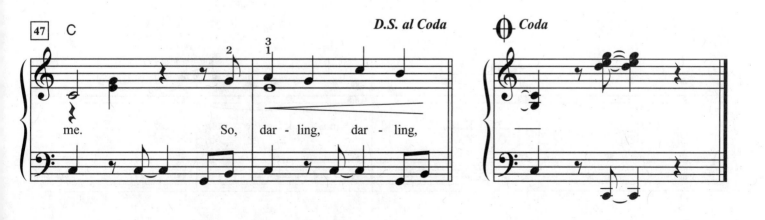

STAYIN' ALIVE

Words and Music by
Barry Gibb, Maurice Gibb and Robin Gibb
Arranged by Dan Coates

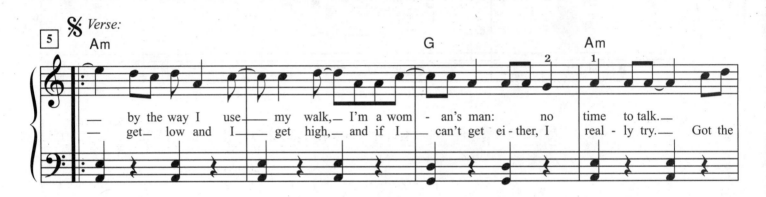

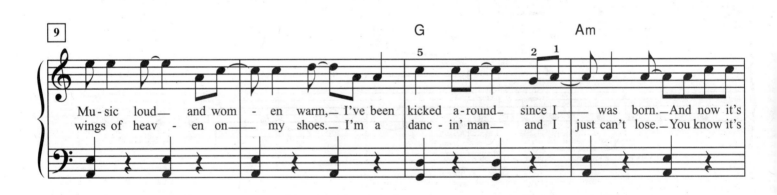

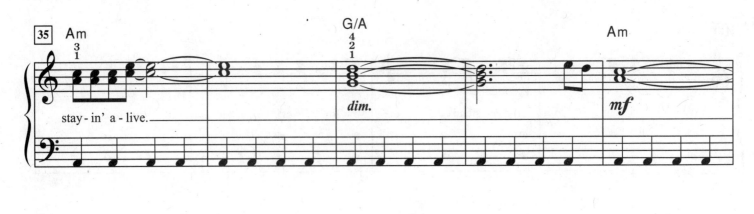

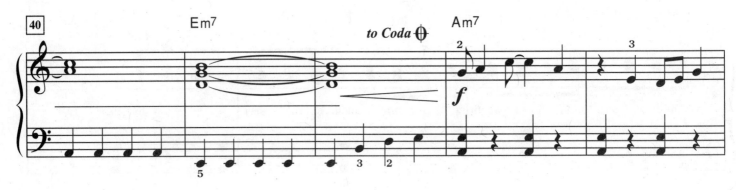

WAKE UP LITTLE SUSIE

Words and Music by
Boudleaux Bryant and Felice Bryant
Arranged by Dan Coates

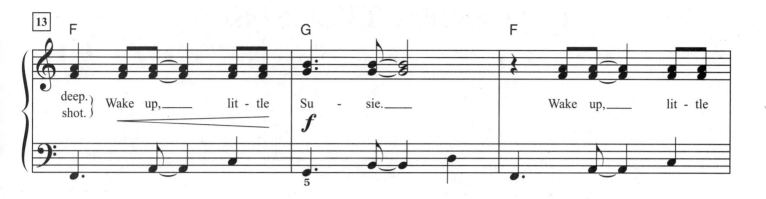

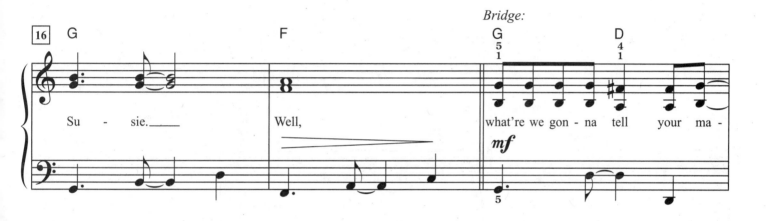

la?" Wake up,_____ lit - tle Su - sie._____ Wake up,_____ lit - tle

Su - sie._____ 2. Well, I told your ma - ma that

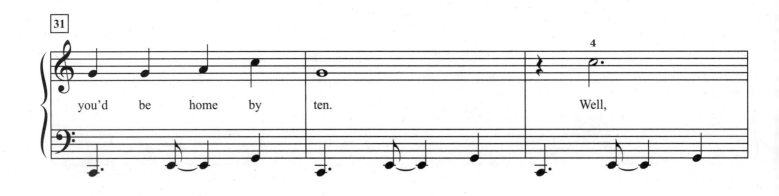

you'd be home by ten. Well,

Su - sie, ba - by, looks like we goofed a - gain._____

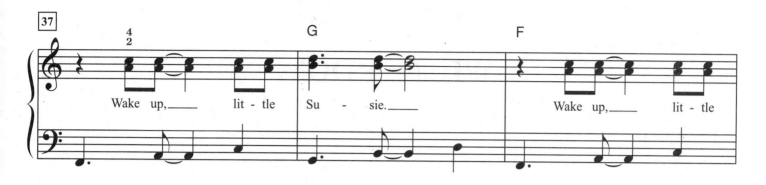

WHITE ROOM

Words and Music by
Jack Bruce and Pete Brown
Arranged by Dan Coates

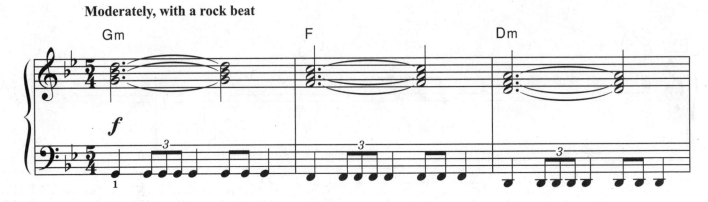

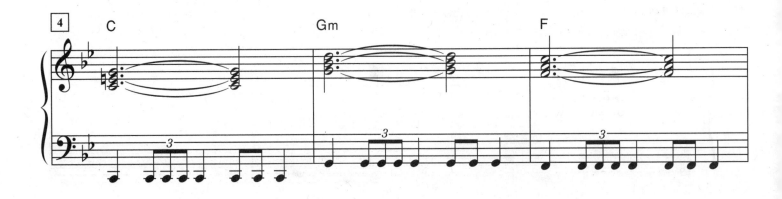

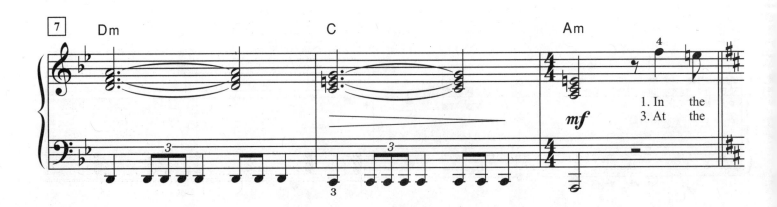

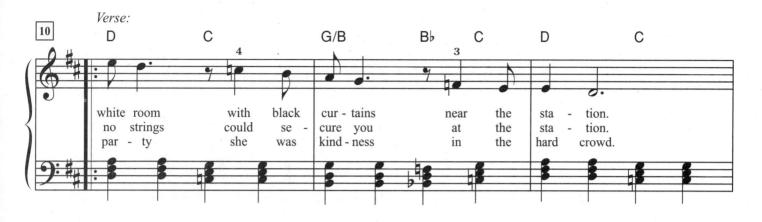

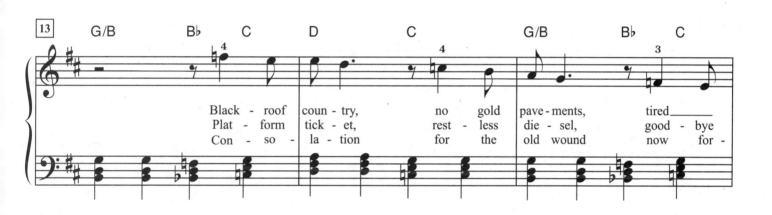

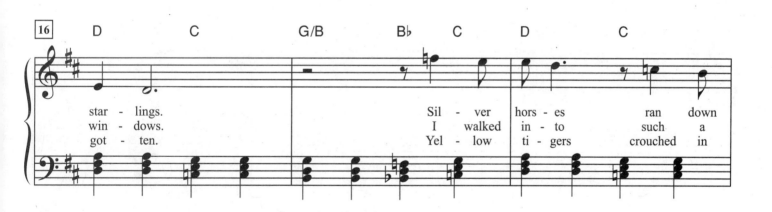

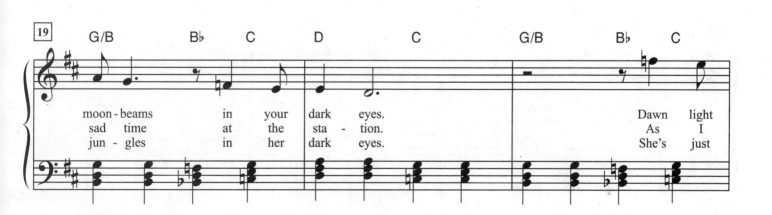

136

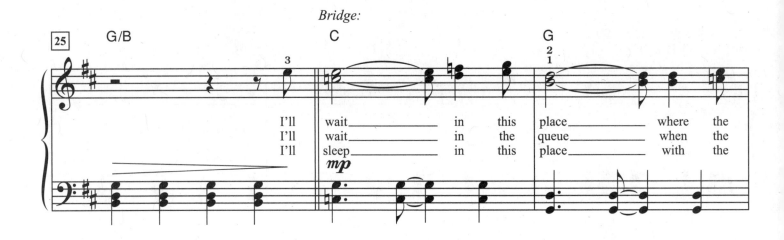

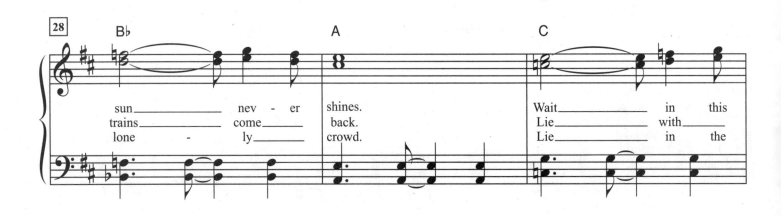

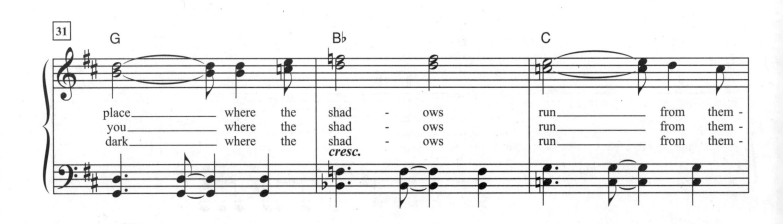

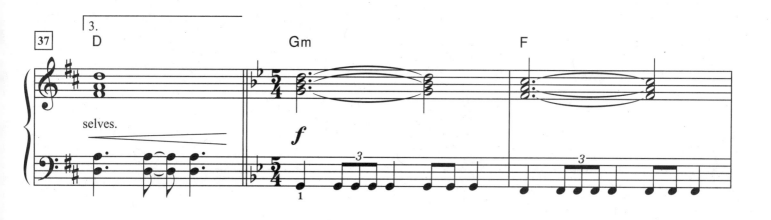

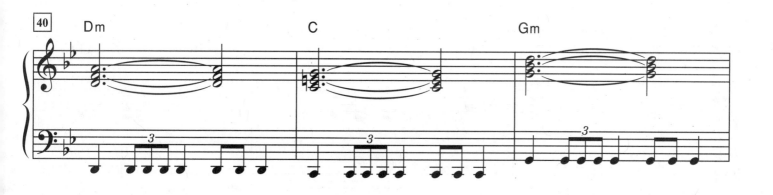

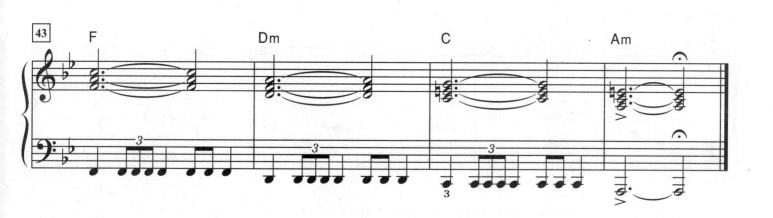

A WHITER SHADE OF PALE

Words and Music by
Keith Reid and Gary Brooker
Arranged by Dan Coates

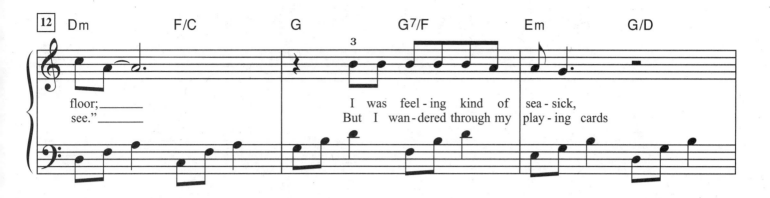

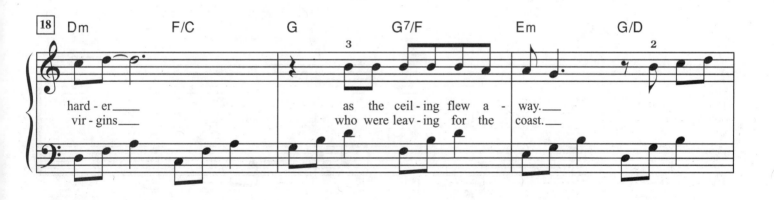

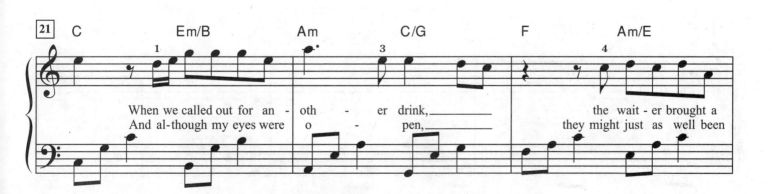

Chorus:

24 Dm7 — G — C — Em/B — Am — C/G

tray.
closed.

And so it was_____ that lat - er,

mf

27 F — Am/E — Dm7 — F/C — G — G7/F

as the mill - er told his tale,_____ that her face, at first just

30 Em — G/D — C — F — C — G7

1.

ghost - ly, turned a whit - er____ shade of pale._____

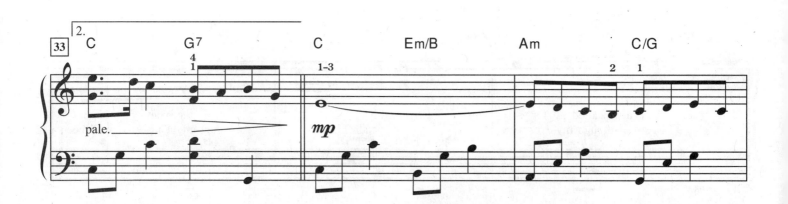

2.

33 C — G7 — C — Em/B — Am — C/G

pale._____ *mp*

WILL YOU LOVE ME TOMORROW

Words and Music by
Gerry Goffin and Carole King
Arranged by Dan Coates

but will you love me to - mor - row?
Will you you still love me to - mor - row?

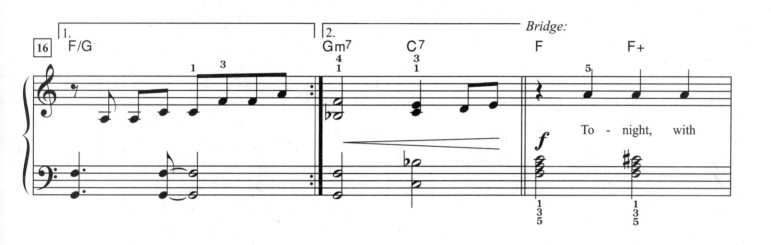

To - night, with

words un - spo - ken,

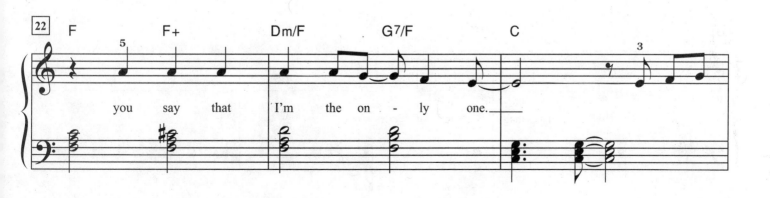

you say that I'm the on - ly one.

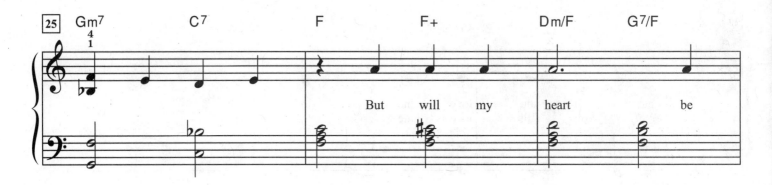

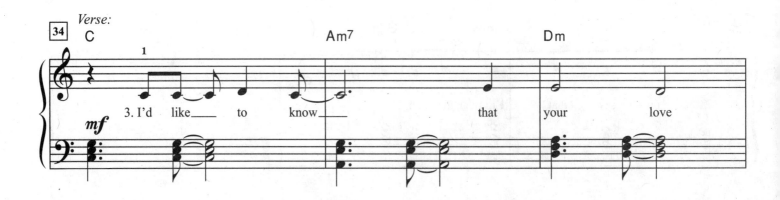

THE WEIGHT

Words and Music by Robbie Robertson
Arranged by Dan Coates

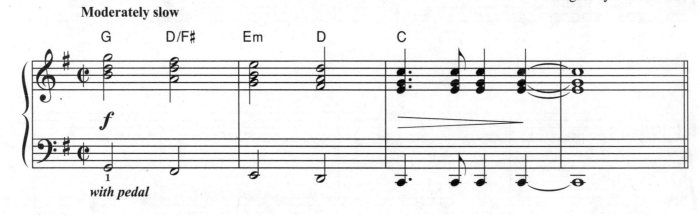

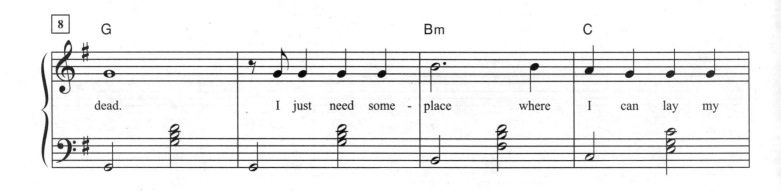

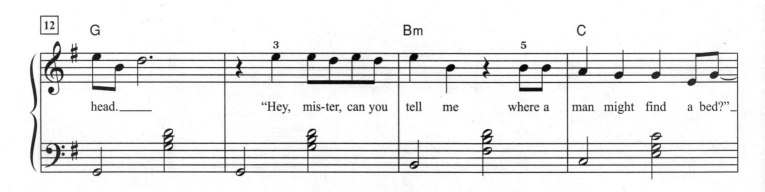

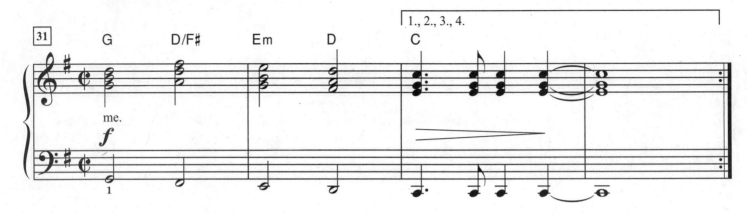

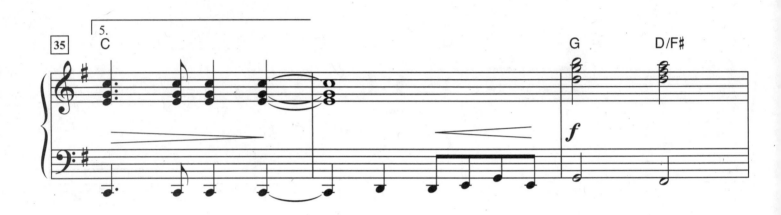

Verse 2:
I picked up my bag, I went lookin' for a place to hide,
When I saw Carmen and the devil walkin' side by side.
I said, "Hey, Carmen, come on, let's go downtown."
He said, "I gotta go, but my friend can stick around."
(To Chorus:)

Verse 3:
Go down, Miss Moses, there's nothing that you can say.
It's just old Luke, and Luke's waitin' on the Judgement Day.
I said, "Luke, my friend, what about young Anna Lee?"
He said, "Do me a favor, son,
Won't you stay and keep Anna Lee company."
(To Chorus:)

Verse 4:
Crazy Chester followed me and he caught me in the fog.
He said, "I'll fix your rack if you'll take Jack, my dog."
I said, "Wait a minute, Chester, you know I'm a peaceful man."
He said, "That's okay, boy, won't you feed him when you can."
(To Chorus:)

Verse 5:
Catch a cannonball, now take me down the line.
My bag is sinkin' low and I do believe it's time
To get back to Miss Fanny,
You know she's the only one
Who sent me here with her regards for everyone.
(To Chorus:)